MW00653261

A
Practical Guide
for Building
Wealth

Kevin J. Daniels

© Kevin J. Daniels

ISBN: 978-1-54394-433-4

All rights reserved. This book or any portion thereof may not be reproduced or used in any
manner whatsoever without the express written permission of the publisher except for the use
of brief quotations in a book review.

CONTENTS

DISCLAIMER

I am not an attorney, nor an accountant, and certainly am not claiming to be one. I have observed many attorneys and accountants and their suggestions, but this book is merely helping you ask YOUR accountants or YOUR attorney to explain this subject in more detail. This is a light brush on monetary subjects to start the thinking process. Please never use this book as anything more than a starting place in your decision process. Information contained herein is based on sources and data believed reliable, but is not guaranteed. This is for illustrative purposes only and not <u>indicative of any investment</u>. This material is not intended to replace the advice of a qualified attorney/tax advisor. Before making any financial commitment regarding the issues discussed here, consult with the appropriate professional advisor. Investacorp, Inc. and its affiliates are not responsible for the accuracy and authenticity of this material. Securities by licensed individuals offered through Investacorp, Inc. A registered Broker/Dealer. Member FINRA, SIPC

DEDICATION

And As For My Beautiful Editor (My wife Lisa):

Lisa is my best friend and my one and only companion. She never stands in the way and has faithfully followed me through whatever crazy idea I dreamed. She has plenty of opinions and is considerably smarter than me, (which puts me at a severe disadvantage when we disagree), but she is faithful and lets me lead. We have laughed, played, cried, worried, celebrated and loved together through life with six children, two dogs, fish, hamsters and even a hedgehog and now grandchildren. She is what the Bible calls the "Proverbs wife". Once upon a time we were too prideful and stubborn to admit we were going to profoundly mess up all of our lives if we didn't change. Thank God we came to our senses and altered our behavior to the better before we got a divorce. I did not realize at the time how significant that was financially. One of the first laws of wealth is this: when you divide your estate through divorce, you end up with less than you had together. I cannot tell you how glad I am that we worked it out. I have made it abundantly clear that if she ever decides to leave this marriage, I'm going with her! Over thirty years later, I can't wait to get home in the evenings to see her again. I call her everyday from work, even when I have nothing to say, I just like to hear her voice. I'm crazy about her!

CHAPTER 1

MAKE CERTAIN YOU ARE PREPARED FOR WEALTH

(BECAUSE IT SOLVES SOME PROBLEMS AND CREATES OTHERS)

Wealth Is Not For Everyone

Money seems to be one of those things that so many desire to possess in greater abundance, yet statistically few actually accomplish the goal. Most Americans will never meet with a financial advisor or even understand what they do. Some do grow very wealthy over time and some seem to slip further down the debt slope or just scrape by most of their lives. Much of America is not prepared for what comes next.

Money can change the state of a human being. It can air condition your house if you are hot or deliver a pizza to your door if you are hungry. Money can afford you the great feeling that comes from helping a friend, charity or family member over a difficult obstacle. Money repairs your car if you are stranded on the side of the road or sends your child to college. Money will put you on boards and make your ideas mean something. It can cause people to sit up and take notice when they would otherwise not. Money can solve certain problems and create others. Warren Buffet is treated as an action hero because he has learned some of the laws of wealth, and has practiced them routinely. I once saw a bumper sticker that said "Money will not buy happiness...but it will rent it!" Money will not bring happiness; that comes from elsewhere.

It Can Be Done

You do not need a big salary to accumulate wealth. Ponder that sentence because most people don't believe it to be true. Any local financial office will have no shortage of stories about people who have earned six times the average household income for twenty-five years and then have next to nothing for retirement. Any experienced advisor can point to people who had every financial advantage known, yet live their retirement years at poverty level. Over the years I have watched as struggling single moms who had little grow very rich. I have seen divorcees roll up their sleeves later in life and build considerable wealth. Our office has witnessed people who were homeless as teenagers come to our offices in their twenties to invest what most people would refer to as a lot of money. We all have heard stories of immigrants who landed in America without speaking English and having five US dollars in their pocket, go on to build companies that would better be termed empires. We have been first hand witnesses to this fact over and over. Still, it is the exception, not the rule. It can be done, yet very few do so.

Wealth is a Choice, So What Do You Choose?

The absence of money, the inconvenience of being inconvenienced by a lack of money, or the outright struggle that comes from poverty can often be the catalyst that propels us forward or the thing that sends us over the edge. I like what my friend Richard Minervino, CEO of the Minervino companies said, "I am so thankful I was born poor". I think he was saying that his poverty fueled his desire to press forward and gave him the energy and diligence to make things different. Personally, I remember as a young teenager watching my grandfather attempt to glue a cracked fish tank back together so he could try to enjoy his precious fish. I remember thinking, "I never want to be forced to live this way". It did not bother my grandfather to live life that way. He did not really desire more. I remember sitting in the kitchen one day when he returned from a thrift store with a pair of boots that were very inexpensive because although the same style and size, one was black and one was brown. He wore them often and was not troubled by this oddity. Not everyone desires money or what it can create.

Money Caution

Money, can be used for good or evil as well. A gun can be used to protect the innocent or kill the innocent. Explosives can be used to crush rock and build roads or they can be used for terrorism. More accurately, the love of money can drive you to ruin. The love of money can make humble folks arrogant and unlikeable. Such love can change you into a miserable miser or even worse, a dishonest person or a thief. Al Capone, Bonnie and Clyde and Jesse James all discovered that the love of money leads to ruin, just like the Bible said thousands of years before they were born. Like nearly anything on earth, good or evil can be produced from the same bowl.

The Greatest Book On Finance

The greatest book on finance that I have ever read is the Holy Bible. People may raise an eyebrow when they hear such a statement, but it really is true. The Bible is actually a collection of sixty six different books that are very ancient but as correct today as when they were written. There is no single book in the Bible that is dedicated to money, but rather hundreds of references woven into the pages. What I like about this mysterious text is that it is always correct on every subject and that includes finance. I have never found the Bible to be wrong, although I have tried many times, unsuccessfully, to prove otherwise. My frequent differing opinion on how the world should work proves no contest to those writings; they have survived millennia, they were here before we were born, and they will be here after we are gone. If I need a 100% guaranteed right answer on any life subject, I always turn to the Bible, and financial answers are no exception. I may not care for the instruction, but it will be right and it will work. Everything in this book stands in the shadow of the Bible and harmonizes with the Bible.

Identifying Trends

How very fortunate I am to honestly say, I love my job. My tasks are diverse and ever changing. The days simply vanish away because in general I am so focused on helping people, I lose track of time. In finance, you never can know it all, for there is too much, which makes constant learning a must. It stands to reason that when we perform a task routinely, we get better at accomplishing the task.

Most financial advisors over time turn into counselors, salespersons, life coaches, encouragers, voices of reason, and dispensers of common sense. They have to be. Money is at the heart of every household and marriage. Advisors sit in meetings with one client after another hour after hour, day after day, year after year and they get to know folks and their families and their financial habits. They sit in one meeting with someone crying and fifteen minutes later are with someone telling jokes. The advisor has to listen carefully to the client so that they ultimately can know what is most suitable for whoever is sitting across the conference room table. Unlike the doctor that spends a few minutes with a patient, or an attorney that may not see a client for years, the financial advisor has the precious luxury of spending hours with clients year after year often spanning family generations. Serving three family generations simultaneously is not unusual. This affords the advisor the ability to spot financial trends, effortlessly.

Those trends would take months to teach in the classroom or pass onto a client at a time, hence this book. I have observed the wealthy in action for many, many years and have tried to compile some of their habits and thinking in the pages that follow. In general I punt when it comes to reading books. I prefer technical articles and papers that get right to the point. Outlines, paragraphs with headings, and summaries seem to allow a reader to be more effective at picking and choosing which part of a book they will explore; and that is exactly what these articles were written to do…"To get right to the point". Use this book like a tool. Underline and scribble in the margins. Start with Chapter 6 if that's what you desire. Create your own index on the pages in the back so you can reference a topic quickly until it becomes a habit. Please remember that neither of us is complete in our learning. Some days it seems as though I have just scratched the surface of what I could know about the art, science and practice of managing money.

Like So Many Things, This Began As Something Else

The new Advisor In 1998

Starting out as a young advisor is difficult. You need an outlet to be noticed and a chance to show you are worthy of handling someone's money. For me, writing a financial column seemed like it would accomplish the goal. After being turned down by the bigger newspapers in town (since I was not a union journalist), I looked for any outlet to publish a column. Tony Brockmeyer was a calm, but outspoken man that walked the streets of St. Charles, Missouri with a camera. Almost daily he was looking for something to write about. He never seemed to move fast enough to publish a weekly paper, but it was always ready to go to press by the deadline. Perhaps Tony always wanted to publish a newspaper where he could print whatever he wanted, however he wanted, (because that's what he did). He started the First Capitol News (on First Capitol Street) right about the time I was looking for a paper that would publish a financial column. I was starting out and so was Tony's paper. He was proud to be a free thinker and he was just the kind of person to take a chance on a young guy who "said" he could write a financial column, but had never written a financial column and who "said" he was a financial advisor,

5

but worked out of a converted broom closet in the back of an musty old building. Tony probably knew it was a long shot, but after talking him into a test run article, my "Money Talks" column began to be published in the First Capitol News. Most of these articles were first unveiled in that small home town newspaper in St Charles, Missouri, where as of this writing, some 15 years later, it is still being published by Tony and his team. The articles were meant to be quick and pointed and simple enough for anyone to understand with a little effort.

I will never forget the day that I came to the office and bent down to pick up my copy of the First Capitol News only to find that Tony had printed my picture on the entire back page of the paper! I called the news office and said, "What are you doing, Tony?" He replied, "People need to know who you are. What better than a life-sized picture in the First Capitol News". He chuckled.

Eventually Tony trusted me and stopped proofing my articles and simply published them whenever he needed a column. Week after week I would see something that clients were struggling with or did not understand. I would scribble down the basics in the car at a stoplight, later in the evening turn it into a one page fact filled lesson on wealth, get a draft to my wife who would shred them with red ink. I would re-edit, fax them to the compliance department, get a staff member to make the correction and then pass the completed article to the First Capitol News.

As you begin to read this book you may feel like you have read a passage before in another chapter. One of the ways we learn is through repetition and since this column was published for years, the same concept may be discussed in similar terminology. You may also notice some of the numbers, figures, interest rates etc. are dated because of their original publication date. Regardless, this is not a novel, it is a handbook and if you can abandon the story and grasp the concept, you will have learned the principal behind the wealth generation. Sadly, I sometimes do not take my own medicine and catch myself breaking those guidelines and then paying the price later on.

I Am Really, Really Rich

Think of the actors, actresses, superstars, executives and all of the famous people who had more money than they could possibly spend yet lived an unhappy life or may have eventually taken their own life in desperation. We often think when they have everything (that money can buy) why are they so miserable? Remember that money will not make you rich, let me explain. We no longer have a kitchen table and that is by design. A few years ago we bought a different house and chose not to have a kitchen table. This means we go into the dining room or on the patio to eat. The dining room is a bigger room and it is a nicer atmosphere than the kitchen. The patio table allows a casual restaurant feeling where we are together. It makes dinner more social and less of a filling station. So when the table is full with friends and family and neighbors gathered around, and there is laughter, teasing and lots of big stories flying through the air along with the passing of the potatoes, I look at Lisa and say "This is what makes us really, really rich!" She agrees.

Chapter two and beyond will give you short clips into changing your money habits over time. They are each a quick read that will present a money concept that you might want to enact in your household.

CHAPTER 2

THE CROWD WILL LEAD YOU OFF OF THE CLIFF

*W*hy is it that so often we are comforted when we do as others are doing? Are we unsure of our own decision making, or are we comforted by others making decisions for us? Do we find that we are justified if everyone else is doing "it" even if "it" is the wrong thing to do in the first place?

The long line at the ticket window must be the correct line because, after all, everyone else is standing there. What do they know that I have not discovered? Few people will go to another window and attempt to form a new line. However, if the brave one at the new window gets serviced, after a period of time, people will migrate and form that second line, but, usually only after someone else has led the way.

There is a famous story about sheep in Istanbul Turkey following the crowd. Major world newspapers and media covered a story in 2005 of a sheep jumping off of a cliff and 1500 other sheep followed, right off the cliff! About a third of those sheep died in the jump. There was nothing the shepherds could do. The sheep *just followed the crowd and kept jumping. It must have seemed like the right thing to do for a sheep. And so it is with finance. The crowd will lead you off of a cliff! Beware of the water cooler discussions of grand returns with little effort and no risk. The crowd will lead you off of the cliff.*

Most of the articles in this book are at least inspired by events that we have been privy to or events that have happened right before our eyes. We say in our offices, "You just can't make this stuff up" and "Her car was as clean as a whistle…" is a classic case. I will never forget the day I watched this true event unfold. My only involvement was to write it down!

Her Car Was As Clean As A Whistle…

…new and very stylish. She looked nice too. Neat, clean, well-dressed with a current hair style. As she reached out to get her debit card out of the automated teller, the diamonds in her rings caught the evening sun and I could see that her hands had been recently manicured. She was the very picture of monetary success. Then she zipped away into the sunset, probably escaping to a fine restaurant for a lavish evening of luxury. That's when I pulled forward and noticed her ATM receipt was still in the machine, helplessly rippling in the breeze! What was I to do? She was nowhere in sight. I removed the receipt so I could make room for mine to print. I had to look! She had a balance of $11.94 in her account. Well she *could* have been very wealthy. Maybe this was her 19th checking account that she only used on special occasions. Or maybe she had a $52,000 check that would clear tomorrow. Yeah right! What do you think? I'm guessing that this was her <u>primary</u> checking account and she only had $11.94 left. I think she was like so many who live right on the edge. Missing one paycheck could cause financial disaster.

I remember my grandpa said in the 1950's they would drive through a small town and roll up the windows on the car in the middle of a hot August day to *act* like they had air conditioning! They wanted to give the appearance of wealth. I think this lady at the ATM would have done the same, had she been driving in the 1950's. We all like to give the appearance of financial success, but living above our means is a dangerous game. It is a game with little tolerance for error. How long could you hold out if you missed this week's paycheck? Planning for the unexpected financially speaking is just good sense. A wise fella once told me, "Never live as good as you can afford to".

So how about you? Are you living on the edge? If so, I recommend these tips: Get a plan, start small, and keep at it. If you can afford $50 spend only $40. If you can afford $1,000, spend only $900. Look at your expenses, what could you give up? Ask yourself questions before you purchase something. Can I live without it? If I still want it in six months will it still be there? Could I buy a different one that costs less? Most everyone could live on a little less. We just get in those bad financial habits of impulse or recreational shopping and it's hard to break them. The extra financial cushion will come in very handy some day. I often talk to people that feel the debt closing in around them and they want to make drastic cuts. But drastic cuts can make life unbearable. Instead, I recommend trimming small amounts here and there. And, as always, start today, right now. Start working toward a better financial position. Eventually you'll be glad you did.

PS. Sometimes the rich speak in terms of "staying power" meaning how long they could survive in low-income times. Increasing your "staying power" will help you sleep better and worry less.

Really Bad Financial Advice...

This is the kind of advice your very chatty relatives give you at the family reunion after you have had a big meal and would really like to go to sleep. They give you their top pearls of wisdom concerning finance, which may sound something like this: (Remember this crazy advice is coming from your chatty relatives!)

1. Only listen to people in New York. They get financial information first, and when they are done with it, they put it on TV.

2. Bury money in jars. This way it never gets lost in a down market.

3. Most people do not get scared of market ups and downs, only market downs. That is why they should sell when it is down.

4. Put all your eggs in one basket. That way if you pick a winner, you will get really rich, really quickly.

5. Don't worry about saving money until you are rich. It will be a lot easier because you will have more money to save after you are rich.

6. Predicting the future is pretty easy. Just listen when you are around their friends, they generally have an opinion about the future.

7. When you pick a stock, just look for a company that you feel is doing very well. Gut-instincts are usually right.

8. Ignore tax strategies. Since everybody has to pay taxes, we are really all in the same boat.

9. You can make a fast profit by buying stocks and selling them quickly. A nephew's neighbor's son did it a couple of times, or so they heard.

10. It is really easy to buy low and sell high. They (the relatives) did it a couple of times personally. It's so easy that most of their friends have been very successful at it.

11. When you lose money in the market, make a list of all the things you could have bought with the money you lost. Whine to anyone that will listen and after that, sell what ever is left.

While these are completely satirical, many people will read them and be confused as to why they are NOT sound advice. Each is based on a common theme we have heard from potential investors. Usually without understanding financial concepts, they implement the same errors over and over. Can you find any on the list that seem out of place? Keep reading and we will explore these concepts over time.

Got Investa-gestion?

Monday Morning: Client says, "I want to use this money for retirement. I will not need it for a long time. I don't want to think about if for at <u>least</u> 10 years."

Tuesday Afternoon: Market goes down.

Wednesday All Day: Client panics and spends the day in miserable worry as if the sky is falling.

Thursday Morning: Client says, "I am so stressed, I know my account must be decreasing. Move me to a cash position!"

Friday Morning: Market goes up significantly.

Friday Afternoon: Client says, "I should have stayed in!"

One Week Later: Repeat.

Sound familiar? Investa-gestion I call it. Market timing is really what they are attempting, and I do not know a single soul that would recommend individual market timing. Since their money is very important to them, they are miserable when it goes down. Are they investors? Maybe not. Savers and investors are different. If you worry about your money, are constantly checking your account, or have plain ole investa-gestion then try these ideas.

Idea #1: There are many fixed-rate products for savings. Secure a rate that you are comfortable with and sleep like a baby at night. The big disadvantage here is that inflation and taxes can erode that nest egg. For example how much was a gallon of milk when you were a baby? A lot less than it is today! The advantage of a fixed rate product, is that it may be very consistent, but what about the inflation? Obviously, the longer the time horizon, the higher interest rate someone is willing to pay. Examples would be: fixed rate annuities, certificates of deposit, and bonds.

Idea #2: Go to prudent investments. Stay well diversified and make sure you use low volatility type strategies. The key is getting a good mix. Diversification really works! More prudent examples might be government bonds, utility stocks, blue-chip (large) corporate stock, treasury bills, and fixed rate annuities. For more diversification, try a mutual fund. Nearly every investment company will have literature that clearly ranks their funds and discloses their unique risks.

In Summary: I don't believe the average person can save their way to prosperity. I believe they have to invest their way to prosperity. But, when the markets take a dive can you handle the stress? I suggest that if it bothers you to see the dive, then take a lesser performance choice and sleep well. After all, you will have saved money on your medical bills because you have cured your investa-gestion! (Before you invest, please speak with a financial professional who can help educate you on the key concepts involved).

Advice From The Richest Man In The World

... Or at least he was a couple of thousand years ago. His name was King Solomon, and at the time he ruled over the most powerful nation in the world. He wrote this: "A man who wants to get rich quickly will fail." I see people's tax returns. From what I see on those returns, I think he is right! Tax returns have a way of "blowing the whistle" on get rich quick schemes. So many gamble tens of thousands of dollars on every instant money idea imaginable; half-baked business start-ups, lottery tickets, network marketing schemes, pyramid marketing networks, real estate gimmicks, horseracing, and every sort of high-risk speculation the mind can conceive. All these schemes are designed to help you get rich quick (just like they were in King Solomon's day).

Now don't get all worked up here. This is about finance. So if you are looking for the perfect get rich quick idea, consider Solomon's advice. It's been played out many times over the last two thousand years. I believe all of the above methods have a common theme: Lack of good information and unfortunately, information gathering takes time. Consider this. When a client comes into my office and says they want to buy stock X, my first question is: why? Usually they will say it's because they think the company's product is good and therefore the stock price should increase in the future. Companies with extremely good innovative products fail every day in America. What happens? Obviously, their success is not dependent <u>only</u> upon their products. We need more information to decide if the venture is worthwhile. Not every bad investment is immediately recognizable. However, knowing little or nothing about it is a sure recipe for problems. Another example: I see people with really good intentions decide in one evening to start a new business. They quickly rent a location, buy all of the business tools and quit their previous job. But they may not have spent enough time in the information step. They failed to read on the subject, or to review the statistics. They failed to research the idea adequately or even create a business plan. They just jumped in, usually by spending a lot of money up front. They had good intentions, but seem to have gotten caught-up in the idea of success or having a change of pace or being their own boss, or buying "business stuff" instead of researching the steps that lead to that success. Yes, they lack information! America has information everywhere: government hotlines, books, pamphlets, the internet, public service agencies, consultants, and libraries and so on, most of which are free.

So you have a plan to make money, great! Start your research. Make a list of all the places you can find information about your idea. Read everything you can on the subject and talk to people who have been successful using the same plan. People that are not competitors will share freely. Read several books on the topic. Go to seminars and ask questions. If at the end of your study you still believe your money-making strategy is correct, all the better! It's much easier to stay on the correct financial path, when you have adequate information.

PS. Making money is fun, but I propose a NON-get rich quick way. It's boring, slow, mechanical, and makes a very dull story at your next party, but it is effective! Stash away a little money at a time. You may want to use a part of your tax refund, part of a bonus, or a raise. Mechanically put this money to work in a solid venture. It is not very exciting, but it will force you to save and it will add up before you know it! Thanks King Solomon.

There is never a shortage of families that earn significant incomes for decades at a time, yet have almost no net worth. They have no investable assets, no real equity in real estate and can often even have mounds of debt. Sometimes we ask ourselves, "what do these people do with so much money?" To this day, this is a mystery to me.

Couples Retirement Plans Robbed!

Have you heard about the recent phenomenon where couples are having their entire retirement plans robbed...of all funds? People in Denver, Chicago, New York, Los Angles and now St. Louis have been affected. These folks both young and old alike are having their future financial well-being robbed by credit card balances! Families with stable high paying jobs are sending their retirement funding to credit card companies for interest on cappuccinos, cigarettes, restaurant dinners, clothes, concert tickets, cell phones and every sort of expenditure imaginable. Unfortunately, what these people are experiencing is that all of their (would be) seed money for their retirement savings is going to pay credit card interest. They are paying interest on items often purchased years ago, some of which have already been sent to the garbage dump. They *want* to build their retirement fund but are paralyzed by credit card interest. If you fall into this category read on. Here are some possible solutions:

Remember, generally speaking, there are only two ways to reduce debt (or credit card balances) earn more or spend less.

Get a temporary second job and use <u>all</u> of the income to pay debt. This is a more popular alternative than trying to cut the expenditures in the household budget. It is inconvenient, uncomfortable, time consuming and not very fun. But it certainly is one way to earn cash to retire credit card debt.

Go cut up the credit cards and start using cash today. Cash (from the bank where there are no withdrawal fees) is a cumbersome inconvenience compared to that piece of plastic we call a credit card. Cash forces us to realize just how much we spend. And most of all, you cannot spend cash unless you have cash to spend.

Use a consolidation or home equity loan. Be careful, this can be the beginning of financial recovery or the beginning of a bigger financial black hole. If we are disciplined, a home equity loan with a lower rate can eliminate the higher credit card interest. If the newly "zeroed" cards are used again, the financial condition is only worsened.

Look at the interest rate. Often people will say "Should I pay down my highest interest card first?" Yes, if your card balances are all about the same. Another strategy is to pay the lowest balance first. It is good to be encouraged by progress.

Seek professional help immediately. So many times folks do not want anyone to know that they need help. By the time they do ask for help, they are in deep. Seek credit counseling quickly. There are many local organizations dedicated to helping individuals who are being swallowed by debt.

Transfer your high interest credit card to a zero percent card for a period of time. I believe this can be effective provided you continue to pay the same amount you would have had you still been paying the higher interest. Also, read the fine print and know the written rules of the game. Six months or a year at no interest can really make a dent in that debt. But take the time to understand the details of this type of card. No doubt that company offering a zero percent interest is making an attempt to gain your future business. Be careful with this one.

Notice I did not mention bankruptcy. This is a very last resort in my opinion. Bankruptcy will haunt you for many years if not for the rest of your life. I am told that many choose this route for a "clean start". I have seldom seen this build one's self esteem, character or really solve the actual financial woe. It is a financial band-aid at best. Avoid it if at all possible.

Sell goodies. This choice is painful because usually one sells goodies for less than you paid for the items initially. A smaller house, older cars, no cell phone, or a reduced plan, no cable television, and eating at home all free funds to be used toward that debt retirement.

No one ever said retiring debt is fun. How badly do you want to be rid of that payment?

Stuck in the Future?

Have you ever noticed someone that looks like they came from a different era? Maybe they use phrases and words that are out dated. Maybe their hair style is retro, their clothing is periodic, or their mannerisms seem dated. It's as if they found a time in their life that they really liked and stayed there. You may have thought "If 1985 ever comes back they'll be ready!" Sometimes they even get a little chiding for getting stuck in the past.

But what about the people that get stuck in the future? What? How can you get stuck in the future? I meet people almost every day that are living in the future. It works like this: Each day they spend a little more than they have. (Just a little though. They wouldn't want to be financially irresponsible or anything!!) This month they went a little crazy. Next month they repent and do better. But then they slip again and the process repeats itself. Then comes the "Sale" or the "Deal". They want it and they buy it…on credit of course. This week's check pays for last week's expenditures. Next week's check will pay for this week etc. etc. etc. I call it getting stuck in the future. What's the problem you say? Simple, you sell your future to whoever writes your paycheck, because without that paycheck (which is already spent) you're in the RED, big-time!

The solution? Start the process in reverse, slowly. Stop living on tomorrow's money. This week spend LESS than you have. Next week do the same, little by little. Start slow and develop new spending patterns that you know will become habits for the rest of your life. With that small excess from each check you can start whittling away at that debt from the past. Having an extra buck in the wallet will put a sparkle in your eye. Then when that big sale comes around again, not only will you feel good about your bargain, you'll know you can pay for it.

Shopping today touts the American capitalistic marketing system at it's best. Talk to someone in merchandising and they will tell you that the acceptable standards for print quality and display have grown tremendously. Excellence in merchandising continues to rise with displays becoming increasingly grand…and it works! We see the young beautiful/handsome model in living color, and we mentally extrapolate to our own life…it works. We WANT to purchase but…

The Borrowing American

Several years ago, the London Daily Express stated across the front page in two inch high letters "BORROWING HAS GONE BALLISTIC." Latest figures from the bank of England showed debts in England were at record levels. Their Consumers Association was begging for people to stop borrowing and start saving. Sound familiar? This may strike all to close to home. There is no room in the financial world for another alarmist, but I have to admit I see this same trend on a much smaller scale right at my conference table, more often than I care to admit. This is not supposed to happen with people of means.

Many household financial plans operate like this: See something and buy it. Correction: charge it, of course. Monthly credit card payment grows. Go shopping and see something else. Purchase something else, although small. Financial strain starts to build. Financial strain compounds next month. Unexpected but necessary expense arises. This may be car repairs, reduced hours, illness etc. Family scrapes every available source of funds to bail out of emergency. They may contact relatives for quick help. More debt incurred because of emergency. Every aspect of life begins to suffer. Worry sets in. Family decides the only solution is to re-finance the house and pay off the debt. Family has a temporary reprieve with new funding. Three months later purchase is charged again. Husband may blame wife and wife may blame husband. Fear sets in. Financial strain can begin to cause the marriage to suffer. Both are depressed. Decision is made to accept overtime, maybe a 2nd job. Marriage may or may not survive. Decision made to file for bankruptcy to get a "fresh" start. A few years later, cycle repeats. If there is any good news here, I would have to say that it is good that we are identifying the problem before it gets any worse. If you are anywhere in this spiral, get help to get out of that cycle quickly!

So what exactly is England (and America) worried about? Simple. They are worried that a run away train of defaults could start as the economic conditions change to less favorable borrowing conditions. <u>Someone</u> has to pay back the debt. When Americans, English, or any other populous ramp-up the borrowing, the staying power of the general population is lowered. Too many of these scenarios, and the country has economic woe. In other words, folks begin living closer and closer to the edge of financial disruption. Don't get me wrong, nearly every good business person I see borrows. Nearly every home on the block has a mortgage or two. Some business people would say, "If you cannot pay cash for an item, you really cannot afford the item". I disagree. Borrowing has catapulted many poor folks to financial freedom. However, this type of leverage is usually well thought out with a very calculated risk. Borrowing (or leverage) is not the problem. Borrowing is often necessary to achieve the financial goal. However, the wrong kind of borrowing can have a chilling end. Financial strain chisels away at many American households. Again, if you are anywhere in that spiral, get help quickly!

PS. There is a book of ancient wisdom called "Proverbs" and it says: "Now the rich rule over the poor and the borrower becomes the lenders slave". Be careful when allowing yourself to be the borrower!

CHAPTER 3

HAVING A PLAN FOR BUILDING WEALTH

*I*t is very difficult to build a house without a set of plans. A manufacturer of cars has a quantity of drawings that seem incalculable. If you wanted to purchase a set drawings for an airplane, it would take a dump truck to carry them. People who build things have a plan. The bigger the project, the more detailed the plan. But, life gets in the way and another soccer game, birthday party, work issue, broken furnace or any myriad of items of life can get in the way and rob you of a plan. Get angry at yourself for not having a plan for the future. Get angry enough that you set aside time to confront that problem and get a fix in place. This is not complicated; in fact it is quite simple when you boil down the technique. This technique actually removes the stress of daily finance. Time is marching on, so start now.

You Can't Win If You Don't Play

Get rich quick schemes do not work well. We all know this fundamental truth. Yet, when you hear lottery or casino in a sentence, you will hear "you can't win if you don't play" not far behind. When we had a tax practice we used to see the 1099-G gambling proceeds stubs. There were plenty of losses to report, but not much in the way of winnings. Year after year people would come in and claim their gambling losses for the tax returns. Look at the odds and make the odds in your favor.

I saw a bumper sticker the other day. It read, "Money talks, but mine only says goodbye!" I found this to be clever, but obviously, we find it funny because we can relate to a situation where we did not fair so well financially. However, I have never met anyone who likes to lose money or continuously erode their hard earned wages.

Enter the gambler. I have a lot of conversations about "the boats", Powerball® or the lottery in one form or another during the conversations at my conference table. Ironically, we do not see much if any from gambling winnings. I'm sure some wins, and some do invest their bounty. But for some reason or another, we see very little of it end up in retirement/savings accounts.

I would never argue how much satisfaction you get from playing the lottery. Many folks seem to live for these moments. <u>But if you are gambling to make money, don't!</u> Here is why: If you look at a lottery brochure with a picture of "Luckyville" on the front you will see some statement like "It's the luckiest place on earth, , and fortune comes your way, and all you need is a little luck and your lottery ticket." Really? I'm confused, If you look at the math I just don't see how that can be. I suspect many listen to the marketing and ignore the fine print.

Missouri's Powerball® statistics will tell you that the odds of winning $5,000 is one out of 502,195! If you take your calculator and divide 1 by 502,195 your calculator will likely give you "error" or a e-6", which means there are six zeros to the right of the decimal point. This is equivalent to 0.0000001 chance of winning. The engineer or mathematician will tell you, "That's zero my friend!" And if you want to win some significant money for that retirement account, say $100,000 you have a one in 2,939,677 chance of success. I would play those odds every day...but only if I were the <u>owner</u> of the lottery. It's safe to say your odds of winning are zero!

A Jackpot might be better called the miracle-pot with the odds being one in one hundred twenty million! (that's 1 divided by 120,000,000.) "But you can't win if you don't play, Kevin", or "Someone has to win. "Yes, this is certainly true. But with those odds you can't win if you DO play. Purchasing that lottery ticket may launch many dreams of what you would do with so much raw cash, and it will surely make great conversation over lunch. But if it is money you want, your finance person will explain the sad mathematical news showing this is not the way. Read the fine print, it is all right there for you to see.

PS. Some states tout that they give a percent of your ticket price to the state's public education programs. I'll just bet the schools would rather have your contribution <u>directly</u> without administrative fees. And that may be tax deductible for you if you itemize and not are subject to percentage of adjusted gross income rules. Jackpot!

Budgeting For Smarties! (PART I)

Surprisingly, I hear a very common question in the conference room from people whose income seems to span a broad range. Here is the question: "Will you help us with a budget?" It follows my explaining that their salary statistically falls into the top incomes of the world to which they will likely reply, "Well it doesn't feel like it!" We all become accustomed to living on what we make and no one enjoys a budget. I think the problem with budgeting is this: <u>It does not work with much longevity for most families.</u> So they fail, or feel like they have failed, when the kids get sick and there is an extra $350 in prescriptions and emergency deductibles that were not "budgeted." Who could have known? And moreover, what are they to do? Forego the child's treatment? Probably not.

This is a two part article on budgeting that I hope helps take the number crunching out of your already busy day. Try this simple idea that allows "on-the-run" budgeting. I believe that you will find it difficult to keep a spreadsheet in your purse or wallet and retrieve it each time you want to know if you can buy a candy bar at the gas station. This "on-the-run" budgeting process uses four categories of spending (budgeting). The categories are: 1) Mandatory expenses 2) Cash Expenses, 3) Savings Expenses and 4) In-The-Hole Expenses. Remember MCSH "mandatory cash saves holes". Under this structure all financial expenditures should fit into one of these four categories. Commit them to memory until they become a habit. Let me explain:

1) Mandatory Expenses: For many this will be the largest category of expenditures. Grab a scrap piece of paper and start adding up everything to which you are already committed to paying or is not optional. In other words, write down expenses for the things that you must have to live. You have likely already made the decisions about most things in this category. For example, the house payment is not optional in most households. It is a mandatory expense that you are going to pay! The electric bill, gas bill, prescriptions, car expenses, gasoline etc. would all be examples of those mandatory expenses or those that are necessities for nearly every one. OK, Side note: While I think you can get carried away with this idea, you may want to consider what I have seen some clients do. They place as many mandatory expenses as possible on credit cards. Why you say? Because these are going to be paid each month in full, regardless, and many credit cards will give you mileage, coupons, purchase points, awards etc.

> *"I think the problem with budgeting is this: It does not work with much longevity for most families."*

Be careful with this one, it can be a dangerous game if the balance is not paid <u>in full</u> each month. (One final note on mandatory expenses: add to your list a provision for savings as part of this category. If you think about for a moment, savings really is mandatory, but the amount is up to you! And you are going to need this when you get to category three.)

2) Cash Expenses: Here's how the cash account works: After we have established our mandatory expenses, we have second tier expenses like lunches, clothing, entertainment, and *literally most other expenses that do not fall into the first tier mandatory category*. We decide in our initial calculations how much cash each person gets for the month and withdraw that amount at the beginning of the month, every month. How much cash you might ask? Well that depends on many, many factors such as savings, needs, upcoming expenses etc., but mostly it is simply what we can afford. The key here is to use cash. The expenses in this category are never credit purchases...never! We use cash and when it is gone, we do not go back to our well (or bank account). We simply spend no more and try to hang on until the first of the next month. It should work like an allowance. When our children run out of money and want to buy something, we simply tell them they must wait until they get their next allowance. We can do the same with our own money as adults.

It is important to realize that this cash may be spent on anything, and we do not have to feel guilty about spoiling ourselves if funding for our luxury comes from our cash account. Since finances seem to top

the controversy list in many marriages, his and her cash accounts remove much of the heated debate about the necessity of expenditures. Consider this: she gets a pedicure even when funds are tight because it comes out of her cash account. He buys expensive game tickets without remorse, because it comes right out of his cash account. (Notice I did not say that, he pays part of the bills and she pays part because I do not advise dividing the marriage, especially over finances.) One more thing, I have found that when funds are tight, this method can actually strengthen the marriage as one partner helps the other during a tough month. Sacrifice is not all bad!

Next week we will look at the other two categories of expenditures. For now, get those numbers together!

Budgeting For Smarties (Part II)

Last week we discussed a budgeting technique that helps take the number crunching out of your already busy day. This simple budget idea allows "on-the-run" budgeting for busy folks. As I said last week *I think the problem with budgeting is this: It does not work with much longevity for most families.* Keeping a spreadsheet in your purse or wallet is difficult to retrieve each time you want to buy a fountain drink at the gas station. This budgeting process uses four categories of spending (budgeting) which are: 1) Mandatory expenses 2) Cash Expenses, 3) Savings Expenses and 4) In-The-Hole Expenses. Under this structure all financial expenditures should come from one of these four. Here is a short re-cap of what we discussed last week:

1. **Mandatory Expenses**: This is the largest category of cash outflows that encompasses those expenses to which you are already committed and that are not an *optional* expenses like a house, the gas bill, the trash collection etc.

2. **Cash Expenses**: Our second tier expenses are cash expenses. They contain *most other expenses that do not fall in the first tier mandatory category.* The key here is to always use the cash allowance for the month. Never use credit for these expenses and try as hard as you can to avoid taking out more for the month. Like a child's allowance, if you are out of money this month wait until next month when you get another allowance.

Now let's pick up with the third tier:

3. **The Savings Account**: Stay with me. Any expense that is not part of the first two tiers, (Mandatory expenses and Cash Expenses) has to next come from savings. A new car, a vacation, a high-definition television, or anything that that was not a part of the first two tiers, MUST come from savings. No savings, no expenditure! Often these are big-ticket items that are less frequently purchased. Now you see why we say the savings component is part of our mandatory expense!

4. **In The Hole Expenses**: This is the "we are digging ourselves a hole" account. This is **borrowed** money for items that are not a necessity. A five bedroom home for a family of two may be handy, but it is hardly a necessity. A new car is gratifying, but a used one may serve the purpose. There may be a time you elect to borrow funds for a purchase that you really cannot afford, just know these expenses are digging a financial hole for your household. If you could afford them they would not need to be purchased with someone else's money. These expenses certainly may cause rough seas for your financial future, so avoid them if you can!

There you have a budgeting process that is not one size fits all. Hopefully it is one that categorizes buying into four simple pieces that do not require a computer analysis to buy a hamburger. I think you may find that under this plan spending is curbed towards the end of the month, and you will think twice about your cash purchases! You may want to give it a go for 6 months or so. If all is working well, give yourself a raise. If you find that money is still woefully short, my guess is those mandatory expenses have long been too big and may require a serious review. Good luck with your new budget!

Dream A Little

I hope you dream, for dreams are the seeds of success. What you dream about is what you think about, and then becomes what you wish for and eventually what you act upon. We become what we dream.

A few years back every corporation in America seemed to be setting goals. Sometimes the President or Chief Executive Officer (CEO) would set goals first. The vice presidents would then set goals to help the CEO meet his/her goals. The manager set goals that built upon the vice president's and so on. And everyone agreed on one thing: They did NOT like to set goals! Maybe in the workplace goal setting is a chore because it is a requirement and not a choice. And of course, you may or may not benefit personally from the goals you are required to set.

But here's an idea! Set some goals of your own. I am constantly asking clients what goals they have set for themselves. Many say, "to be rich" and then laugh. Why do they laugh? Because they don't think they ever will be financially comfortable. If I press a little further, they'll admit they have no goals whatsoever. I like to set goals! And I like to dream, too. I never have accomplished much that didn't start with a dream that turned into a goal.

The exciting thing is that not all, but many of these goals come true and a lot sooner than we anticipate.

Try this at home: dream a little. Pick a small goal that could become a reality, something that is reasonable. Write it down or put it on the refrigerator. Look at it every day and stray far away from things that jeopardize your goal. I read about one family that got a piece of poster board and filled it with pictures that expressed their dreams. They set priorities and realistic time frames for accomplishing them. Everyone was focused. Think about this, wouldn't it be great to have a vacation fund? Set aside money from every check that goes into a special account only for vacations. Better yet, turn it into an annuity of sorts that keeps the principal secure while still providing you a vacation every year from the interest.

You could use a percentage of a bonus or tax return to seed that fund. Maybe you would like to have the funds to take just one class at the community college or at a technical school. Set the time frame, divide the cost to a weekly amount and start working toward you goal. It's exciting. I see so many clients who are so busy with the daily grind, they don't take time to dream.

If you are ready to start dreaming here are some quick parameters you can use for setting those goals. 1) Make them realistic but still a stretch. 2) Set enjoyable and exciting goals, 3) Reward yourself when you reach milestones and when the goal is accomplished. 4) Write them down and put them someplace visible; we need reminders. 5) Set goals for many different areas of your life: marriage, children, family, finances, etc. 6) Start now.

Zig Ziglar once said: "Success is not measured by what you've done compared to others, but compared to what you are capable of doing." Everyone is capable of setting a few goals, and best of all they are also the beneficiary of the rewards.

Each time I glance at this topic, I recall the bewilderment of the graduating class at a public high school where I was speaking. They were beyond certain that they would all very soon be very rich. You and I know that if that happened, they would likely be the first class in history to do so! Their confidence was high, and they had one of the most prized ingredients for financial success: TIME. Yet their knowledge was so very low. I feared not only did they not know the recipe; they really were even unaware that they needed a recipe.

How Much $$$ Will You Need?

I will just be honest right up front, I can not answer that individualized question in this article. I can give you a nudge in the right direction, but no more.

Not long ago I was listening to Dr. Matthew Greenwald, the President of Matthew Greenwald and Associates, a governmental advisor on American retirement issues. He simply said people have no clue of what they will need for funding in retirement. Financial Advisors may applaud his finding!

If you plan to die at the end of the next week, I would not put much time in on this subject. However, If you plan to be around a while, I would put your heart into finding this answer. For many folks Dr. Greenwald is correct. They have no idea, but they act as though they do. For example, how many people do you know who are at or near retirement yet live like a 35 year old executive who is "ramping-up" their estate. They buy new cars, they routintely dine-out, travel, purchase new homes, golf, have two cell phones, motorcycles, cable, and a boat or two! Their grandkids have learned that grandma is a softer sell than Mrs. Clause and one sad face will make any store's cash register ring. Grandma and Grandpa may be spending down retirement accounts assuming they will only have a few years to live. Perhaps they should read this week's obituaries. In general, people do not die young in our country, when you exclude life-style deaths. Medical technology is extending our lives. Heart attacks do not kill people like they used to. In the 1800s a broken leg could kill you. Today hospitals perform tens of thousands of heart surgeries successfully.

For the first time in history we can outlive our money during retirement. Yet, I routinely see retirees spending as though their computers print one hundred dollar bills. We contact clients by phone, send them letters, and have meetings to slow retiree spending. Many will simply reply, "I need (or want) the money," and they continue to withdraw.

Today's 65 year old may well live into their 90's. Their money has to stretch for some time. Never before have folks needed to plan for retirement of 30 plus years.

The Mechanical Millionaire was, like each of these articles, influenced by actual discussions in a client meeting. The young couple was all future at that point. They possessed in great abundance that precious gift we call time but they were nothing out of the ordinary, just regular people living out their lives.

The Mechanical Millionaire

I asked the client, "How much do you spend on lunch each day?"

The answer came back "Usually about $6.00"

Then I asked, "How often do you eat lunch out?"

The answer came back, "Five days a week".

He was 21 years old at the time and had a simple IRA plan at work to which he made **NO** contributions. The employer's plan matched $1.00 for every $1.00 the employee saved, up to 3% of his salary. However, he was young, had no assets to speak of, was just starting out and groceries and rent were higher priorities than saving for retirement of all things. When life is evaporating every dollar, where could he find money to save? Furthermore, why not start the investing process later, when he would be more established, making better money, and closer to needing the money for retirement?

Let's side track for a moment. It almost seems like we all have a little retirement bell that goes off in our heads when we reach 43 to 46 years old. The little bell rings and we start *seriously* thinking about how we will retire. The body looks different, feels different, and our peers also start talking more and more about retirement. We can begin to see that the day will come when we won't want to work so hard. Hold that thought.

Now back to our 21 year old client. Let's run a hypothetical example. If the client took that $6.00 per day lunch money, five days a week, and faithfully socked it away in the company's simple IRA plan until a retirement age of 65, how much would be in the account? This is boring, mechanical investing. If we assume an 8% return on the money, (because he could invest aggressively,) and assume the employer matched the first 3% (common in simple plans,) he would have over 1.2 million dollars for retirement at age 65! Remember this is the cost of lunch or $30.00 per week.** If we run the equation forward and ask how much a 45 year old would need to save each week using the same assumptions, we see the power of time. He would need to save approximately $2,143 <u>each week</u> to accumulate the same $1.2 Million retirement savings! Yikes! Start early!

We can not back-up. But we can change today. The power of compounding is great, but it really needs time to work. Nearly every financial website you see will have these retirement calculators*. And nearly any hand held financial calculator on the market will run these same scenarios in minutes. The specific numbers are fascinating but the concept is priceless. Start now, start small, and work your way up.

**Also remember this is just an illustration, your actual return will vary with market conditions.

*See www.tributefinancial.com

A Tax Law To Get Excited About!

Ask anyone you know how they feel about taxes, and they will almost always say they believe they pay too much in taxes. Probe a little further and that same person will indicate that they enjoy the benefits afforded by the taxes, but ultimately still believe they are too high. I also find that very few people believe taxes are likely to go down anytime in the near future. If you share these same opinions, read on. This assistance now allows you to have a say in the tax treatment of at least some of your money.

Prior to 2010, some families were prohibited from saving inside a Roth IRA* (Individual Retirement Account) because when you tallied their income, as a family, they made too much money. This was particularly troubling to people who had more than one job, or to families who had two above average incomes. They were not able to take advantage of the Roth IRA tax free benefits...until 2010.

Starting in 2010, ANYONE, regardless of income, can convert to a Roth IRA and take advantage of the tax free status that they afford! The income restriction has been permanently repealed.

But the good news does not end there. You can now convert all or part of an existing Traditional IRA, SEP IRA, Simple IRA, etc. to a Roth IRA at any time but you owe the tax due in the year of conversion and be sure to talk with your tax advisor. They will consider tax on all of your IRA's. This is particularly advantageous if you are at the lower end of your tax bracket and can have more income without going to the next tax bracket. It is important to note that regardless of when you elect to pay the taxes, they will be at ordinary income rates, not capital gains.

A quick study of this Roth conversion will reveal that by paying the taxes owed from a source other than the IRA you are allowed to exceed the normal contribution limits. When you use this technique, you can catch-up on many years of contributions, by simply paying the taxes from non-IRA sources. Of course, should that not be an option financially, you can always elect to pay the taxes from the IRA itself. But, you lose the catch-up benefit. In any case be sure to consult your tax advisor first.

If you are planning on using part of your Traditional IRA and you are under age 59 1/2, be advised that there is a five year waiting period for withdrawals after conversion. Breaking this five year period will cause a premature distribution that will trigger a 10% early withdrawal penalty by the Federal government. If you are over 59 1/2, the income realized from a Roth is tax free, never has required minimum distributions (RMDs), and is not used in calculating social security income calculations, or for Medicare Part B pricing.

One final note: If you convert to a Roth IRA and later decide that it was a mistake, you can "undo" your election. This is called a "re-characterization" and can be elected up to the time you file your tax return for the year in which you made the conversion.

Roth conversions are certainly not for everyone. But to high income bracket tax payers, those planning on passing their IRA to a beneficiary, or those who anticipate higher taxes in the future this opportunity may deserve careful attention. Thanks to this new ROTH IRA law, you have choices on at least some of your taxes!

A Roth IRA is after tax money, so the "principal" part or the initial contribution is never taxed. But unlike other IRAs, in a Roth, the "interest" part or the earnings, are never taxed either!

Source: IRS.Gov For more information see IRA publication #590.

Get a Compass

If you cannot articulate your life/household/financial plans off-the-cuff, then you may be in need of a compass. If you don't know where you are going, you may end up somewhere else.

I only had to get lost one time while scuba diving to realize that not knowing where you are can be scary, really scary. There is only so much air, and the ocean is big! I have made up my mind that whenever I am diving, I will always have a compass with me. When I travel to another country, I usually have a small compass in my bag. With no street signs, or street signs that I cannot read, getting lost is scary, really scary. The wrong side of town and a language barrier is not good in my book. But with my compass I can return to my hotel. I believe that the world of finance is no different when it comes to having a compass. Buy one, rent one, hire one, borrow one or get a freebee, but get yourself a financial compass.

Did you ever notice that a compass works in any direction and does not care which direction you are heading? It points you in a direction and keeps you heading that direction. If you follow your compass North, you will eventually end up somewhere in the North! I see many people on a financial hike with no direction, no map, no compass and no intention of getting one. Year after year they meander because they have no compass.

So what are we to do? Chart a financial course and keep heading in that direction. They come in all shapes and sizes. Some are complex, others are simple. You can pay a lot of money for one that is beautifully bound with gold lettering. Most companies I know do not charge any fees for consultations to form a plan. You can even get a fairly comprehensive plan online. Without a course and some idea of how to navigate the course, it seems unreasonable to expect great financial results. Many insurance companies and investment sponsors have on-line questionnaires that you can access free of charge. Many financial advisors will not charge for helping you create a plan to achieve financial independence.

I see too often people with good intentions who have very good jobs with very nice salaries who have trouble buying groceries. These people often live the greatest part of their lives with no plan. Technically, it is never too late to start. But we would all agree as usual, start now, start today. What are you waiting for?

In the hundreds of financial reviews in our offices, we find that a small percentage of clients keep a running inventory of their net worth. Putting figures on the paper helps many people see where they stand financially, and usually financial savvy retirees know their net worth. Review your net worth once a month and then compare each year to previous years. We are all encouraged when we see progress, and without a running total, it becomes nearly impossible to track progress.

Don't be worthless!

We are required to ask clients about their net worth when they come in to discuss financial matters. Frequently, they respond with a puzzled look and respond, "I have no idea." Furthermore, many really don't care to know about their net worth. Well then, if you are happy with your financial status right now or want to live on even less, I agree. Who cares? But for most of the people I see they want to live on <u>more</u> money, not less. And if you want more money then you can't be worthless, net worth-less that is!!

Financial folks call it a balance sheet but don't worry, a balance sheet is simple addition and subtraction. You can create your own balance sheet scribbled on the back of an old envelope. Try this: tear the envelope in half and write headings **"loans"** on one piece and **"what I could sell it for"** on the other. Now, grab all of your account statements and look at what you owe everybody. Write those items on the piece that is entitled "loans." Things like your credit card balance, the house mortgage balance, car loans, and anything you owe someone would be written on the "loan" portion. (If you have a credit card balance, you have borrowed the money, so it is a loan). Then on the "what I could sell it for" piece, write down the value of everything you have. Be conservative because it is really your best guess of what it would bring in an auction, at a garage sale, or sold on the internet etc. Total each of the two columns. Which number is bigger? Hopefully you *own* more than you *owe*. If so, subtract the two numbers. This is your net worth, or the value of your estate if you sold-out completely.

Net worth is defined as the amount by which your assets exceed your liabilities.

In English: The amount "what I could sell it for" exceeds your "loans". If you owe more than you own, oops! That problem needs to be fixed.

I find many Americans don't really understand what is happening to their personal financial picture. I don't believe it is wise to just press on and hope someday you wake up financially secure. Conversely, I've noticed that seriously wealthy people know their net worth. As a matter of fact, they usually come into the office with a written statement of their net worth. Why? <u>Because this is how they track progress.</u> Officers in companies use this method as a barometer of how their company is doing. Unless your net worth is increasing, you are getting poorer by default. If you stay at the same net worth too long inflation will bite into your money and cause it to shrink. So clip this article, figure your net worth, and check your progress at the same time next year.

Tip: Don't be net-worthless! Make up your mind to build that net worth number. Someday you'll be glad you started now! And oh, by-the-way, nearly every financial software program on the market, as well as countless free websites, will allow you to toss the envelope and create a polished statement of net worth.

My mom used to say "Well, son, that's life," meaning there are twists and turns that come your way that are unpredictable and unstoppable. However, if you plan for things that you cannot plan for, then those unexpected "life" things are not so traumatic. Additionally, it is much easier to take a rational approach when you are not knee-deep in the crisis. This takes a good deal of the drama out of the situation, which really helps when you are forced to say "well, that's life."

Financial Fires

Sometimes in an attempt to see how an individual thinks about a particular subject I ask, "If this building were on fire, which would you do?" Then I give them these four options. a) Bust a hole in that wall over there to get everyone out. b) Try to cheer everyone up with a chipper little song. c) Stay very calm and quiet until someone decided the most effective plan of action. d) Look for an evacuation plan to determine the quickest way out. I get all sorts of fun questions and answers but in my mind the point is to have an idea BEFORE the building catches on fire!

How about a financial fire at your house? What would you do? Are you ready? My crystal ball is broken so I find it difficult to predict unforeseen financial woes in my own affairs. So I have a back-up plan (or two.) There is no one-size-fits-all in the financial world, but I believe we all need a safety net. We need something to catch us if we encounter a few of those "money burners" in a row. Examples of money burners may be a job loss, a medical condition, an injury, car repairs, an insurance claim, unexpected taxes etc. Here are a couple of financial extinguishers in case of financial fire:

- Quick Liquidation Money. Money that can easily be turned to cash is usually referred to a "Liquid" in financial circles. This could be a certificate of deposit or non-IRA money that can be quickly turned to cash. A Non-Traded REIT (Real Estate Investment Trust) or raw real estate is NOT a good example of quick cash because it cannot be quickly liquidated, and may not have the ability to convert at all. The same would be true for a classic car, a coin collection etc.

- Cash reserves. I read of all sorts of fancy formulas, but no one knows your expenses and your tolerance for risk like you do. So, look at your expenses and determine how many months of reserves you feel comfortable with, then stockpile cash. Remember, having a lot of cash is expensive because it earns so little compared to other investments.

- Personal Loan. A relationship from a relative or close friend or even a professional contact that has been "pre-discussed" can help you with a temporary loan as a back-up plan. Be careful with this one, it is not concrete and I would only use this as a second tier back-up if all else fails. Remember this may change that relationship if all does not go well.

- Home equity loan or an equity line of credit. This is perhaps the most popular solution. The money is available should you need it, but does not have to be used if not needed. This requires a bit of discipline because it works like credit and spends rather easily! The nice part of this choice is the interest is typically tax deductible, if the loan is against your primary or secondary home.

Of course there are others. In any case remember to think about fire extinguishers (financial ones!) BEFORE the financial fire starts. Procrastinate on this one and you may just lose sleep when you start smelling financial smoke!

Some people refer to this as karma. Some will say "what goes around comes around." Some will say "you reap what you sow." Jesus of Nasareth told this truth far better than I could ever attempt, and long before you and I were alive. And in the usual biblical way, it is still as relevant today as it was the day he spoke those words. It is worth committing these laws of harvest to memory. When you are tempted to stray from your ethics, remember "Money Seeds".

Money Seeds

Every farmer knows that if you plant wheat, you will harvest wheat. Every gardener that expects to harvest tomatoes knows they have to plant tomato seeds or tomato plants. This earth has some laws that repeat over and over. We often hear "You reap what you sow. Some people say, "You will only get out of it what you put into it." We know and believe this but might not see the connection to money "seeds." Stay with me.

I believe there are three fundamental laws for any harvest (including the money harvest.) It's easy to see the laws at work in your garden. They are: 1) We always harvest the same thing we plant, good or bad. Of course, so be careful what you plant! 2) We always get the crop <u>later</u>. Have you ever watched a child plant a seed in a paper cup? They carefully place the soil in the cup, the seed in the soil and the water on top. They rush to perch the little cup on the windowsill. The next morning they are disappointed because there is no sprout. We know better; the crop comes later, every time. 3) One tomato plant can grow enough tomatoes to feed the block. One Zucchini seed can grow enough zucchini to send some home with every friend. We always get more than we planted. Did you ever notice that the first action is on our part? If you don't plant potatoes in the spring, don't expect to have fresh buttered spuds in the summer.

And so it is with our money. Some people wait and wait for their great money harvest, but they have never planted any seed! When do you plant money seeds? Now. Take a little seed money and invest it today. Invest in something that will yield a great harvest of money. Next week plant some more money seeds. The following week, do the same. Keep planting and let them grow. If you want a large money harvest, then plant lots of seed and plant often. Remember that the return will come later, sometimes much later. (Corn and pumpkins have different "days to maturity" you know!) What kind of crop will you get? That of course depends on what kind of seeds you sow and when you sow them.

What are YOU planting?

One of the secret ingredients of wealth generation is time. Yet, as Americans we are quite comfortable with the idea of instant. We are not so good at waiting. But, you <u>become</u> *wealthy; you do not* <u>turn</u> *wealthy. And, to become wealthy you need time. Have you ever noticed when you see that mint condition antique car at the stoplight, it is ikely being driven by a guy with gray hair? Have you noticed that the people on the back of that large boat in Florida are older? (or it's dad's boat!). It takes time to generate and accumulate. We are unable at present to buy or sell time. It is pre-allocated, so we must use it as the precious commodity that it is.*

The Early Bird Gets The...

One of the saddest scenes I view in our office is individuals in their fifties or sixties, who are trying to retire in the near future yet haven't adequately prepared for that day. We always keep tissues in our conference rooms. Often these people have failing health that further contributes to their predicament. They can be scary in their desperation. Some call it "grabbing at straws" because they look for quick fixes. After all, at this point, time is so short. They often tell me they need a very safe investment, with very high returns, something I have yet to find. Furthermore they concede that they cannot stand to see their account ever go down. They want low risk and high reward.

Emotionally, they can only handle market "ups," and big "ups" at that. These are scary people. They may look for reasons to sue, they may become desperate gamblers, and they may become easily irritated by anyone with possessing more. Fear can dominate their thinking because they are pressed on all sides. They often look to blame someone else. They are truly desperate.

There may be no remedy to their problem, and they often turn to government or charity for help. But, I do know that if you still have time, starting early is one of the best ways to prevent one of these disasters.

Try these: (1) Start now. Procrastinate no further, my friend. Go get your purse or wallet and remove some "George Washingtons" right now. Set them aside and then keep reading. (2) Make up your mind that every dollar that finds its way into your hand must be split. A portion goes to your investment and a portion may be spent. (3) Set goals for how much and how often you will apportion. I recommend paying yourself about 20%, and using the other 80% for general living expenses. Even rich people and retirees have to save. Make these habits a way of life from now on. Go on a *money* diet and consume less dollars. (4) Become an early bird for life. In retirement planning an early bird has a real advantage.

Yesterday is gone, today is already here, and tomorrow may never be ours. But if tomorrow does come, we will be ready for it. The best prevention for a late disaster is an early start.

CHAPTER 4

BUYING YOUR WAY TO WEALTH

I believe "Antique Glasses" was the first article to every debut in the First Capitol News. Interestingly, it made an impact and I received calls not about the principal of money discussed here, but where to buy antique glasses. This article is not about glasses; don't miss the point.

Antique Glasses

Periodically a client will comment about my glasses. They sometimes mention their uniqueness and ask where I got them. It was like this:

As I walked through an antique store, I saw a shelf full of old spectacles. Some of them would have made great costume wear. However, I picked up one pair that looked like Dwight Eisenhower should be wearing them and paid $18.00 for them. I really think the clerk was dying to ask why anyone would buy an old pair of glasses with the wrong prescription lenses. Nonetheless, I had new lenses made and wear the glasses often. So, for $18.00 I got frames made of 14 karat gold that I like as well as the designer frames I was wearing at the time.

When I look at the financing of the transaction, the question is: What was the true cost of the $18.00 frames? Well, if Federal taxes are 25% and state income taxes are 6%, and FICA is approximately 15%*, I really had to earn $28.12 to pay for the antique frames. Using the same analysis, the designer frames cost $468.75!!! Ouch! And we didn't even talk about the price of the lenses.

The point is NOT about where to buy your glasses! The point is that when you consider the tax burden of ANY purchase, <u>cutting the cost of an item is better than getting a raise on your paycheck.</u> Yes, this works for a coupon you cut out of the newspaper, an item on sale, or any type of discount whatsoever. Just think of this same example applied to a car, a house, or some other big-ticket item! Wow!

Whenever you make a purchase ask yourself, "Is there some way I can reduce this cost?" Can I find it on sale? Will the owner take a little less? Can I buy a similar item for less? When you figure in taxes…it really pays to buy things cheaper! The tax impact is great. Why not get a paycheck increase this week, by shopping smarter?

PS. The antique glasses did eventually break so I bought a replacement (antique) earpiece for $6.00. Ironically, my designer frames also broke. There wasn't a replacement earpiece even though they are more now, so I paid $35.00 to have them braised.

*From IRS 2009 tax tables MFJ, self employed adjusted gross income of $68,000-$137,300.

Big companies have buyers. Bigger companies have purchasing departments, and they have those people in place to maximize their purchasing power. We all buy, but we all do not buy at the same price. Please remember that once you learn the laws of wealth, you could actually take advantage of someone, which is a serious mistake which backfires. Avoid the temptation; it will surely be short term gain and long term loss. Always strive for a win for you and a win for them. If one wins and one loses, really nobody wins. However, purchasing power, competitive bidding and negotiation have a profound impact on a budget whether it be personal or corporate and the larger the purchase the more important it becomes. Assume there are only three ways to make money in business. 1) Raise the price of the product (which is difficult in a highly competitive market environment) 2) Sell the product faster (large scale operations require far more capital and risk) or 3) Lower the cost of the item (through wise purchasing). Try lowering the cost of items you buy and see what happens to the bottom line.

Own A Business? ...Let's Talk Terms.

Nearly every industry I know has some kind of terms for companies that purchase inventory on credit. Say Sparky's Fire Trucks Inc. sells fire engines to local fire departments. Sparky's receives an order, calls the fire truck manufacturer and orders the truck after the new truck is built, Sparky's will deliver the truck to the fire department. The local fire department could hand Sparky's the payment in full on the day the truck arrives. But the company that manufactured the truck could give Sparky's Fire Trucks Inc. terms of 5%/15, net 30. This means the invoice is due in 30 days, but if they pay in 15 days, they can subtract 5% off the invoice price. If the truck cost Sparky $400,000, his 5% discount would be $20,000 for paying 15 days early! To earn $20,000 interest in 15 days, the simple interest rate would have to be 21.7%! Wow, try to get that interest rate on your company checking account! Take the terms! Even if you borrowed the money for 15 days at 15% simple interest, you still come out ahead (not to mention the interest cost is a legitimate business expense.) Multiply this principle over several invoices and over several months and suddenly this represents some serious savings.

So why do so many business ignore terms? I don't know. I assume that the checkbook balance is too low to make the shorter pay period. If this is the case, give the client a 3% discount for paying early. In this example the fire department would get a discount of $12,000 while Sparky's Fire Trucks Inc. would still shave $8,000 off of the cost after giving the 3% discount. No money is borrowed, and the checkbook can still be on "empty."

This is a very oversimplified illustration, but it shows the principle behind terms. Complications of compounding, borrowing, accounts receivable and cash equivalents can get tricky so review your specifics with your accountant. If your suppliers don't offer terms, call their credit department and ask for them! Terms are a great way to increase the profitability. Many suppliers will have early pay discounts of 5% or more.

Nearly any finance book you pick up will herald the benefits of taking early pay discounts. In a land with increasing competitive pressures, understanding the value of terms is essential. So if you own a business, don't ignore those early pay discounts, because they are like being paid a healthy interest rate. Learn to talk terms!

Before you take on debt, try to envision what your financial life would feel like once you have signed on the dotted line. Some personalities handle this concept well, and others can be tormented by the slightest burden. Once you know your thoughts on unpaid debt, you will have discovered a lot about your personality... and your finances.

Is Leverage a dirty word?

It can be. Nearly everyone uses it, nearly everyone needs it, and nearly no one likes it. Leverage certainly has catapulted many an investor to wealth and is much of the fuel used in the engine of capitalism. Just as important, when a business (or investor) fails, leverage can often be found somewhere in the cause.

Leverage is a financial term that describes in many ways, debt. For example, If I asked you for a $10.00 bill on Monday and gave you $15.00 on Friday, would you do it? Sure, and pretty soon you would be asking me on Mondays if I wanted to borrow another $10.00 bill. If I used that borrowed $10.00 bill to make $30.00 by Friday, I essentially would have used your ten dollars to make a $15.00 profit, even after returning your $10.00 and giving you $5.00 in interest.

Investment Income:	$30.00
Amount borrowed:	($10.00)
Interest paid:	($5.00)
Profit:	$15.00

Leverage. I leveraged ten dollars to make fifteen. Simple right?

Say for example a real estate investor makes an agreement with a lender to borrow money to purchase a property. He then seeks to make a profit either by income from renting the property or by selling it in the future at a higher price. Without leverage (in this case a mortgage), it would be very difficult to save enough cash to buy the property free and clear. Leverage makes the investment possible, but it has more risk. Borrowing money to invest in the market is called margin, but it is really just another form of leverage. A margin account is a "borrowed money account."

In corporations leverage is used to expand the operations. When a company sells bonds, they are leveraging, or borrowing money to expand the operation in hopes of returning a profit. The accounting may be complex, and the numbers may be in millions, but the concept remains the same. When companies (and investors) keep the watchful eye on the debt to equity ratio, they are really watching how much leverage there is compared to how much the company actually owns. If the company owned nothing and borrowed everything, then what incentive would there be to try? (This is why you are required to have a down payment on your house.) With little or no equity, the chance of default is too high. Therefore, the risk would increase and no one would buy their bonds. The lender, whoever they may be, wants to make sure the borrower has a stake in the investment! Leverage is a delicate balance. Too little means, opportunity can be lost forever. Too little can render expansion impossible. Too much can make profits small. Too much can eat away years of earnings. Too much can cause the house payment to be unbearable. Too much can bring default! In tough times, leverage often becomes a "ball-and-chain".

In the future, start looking at the amount of leverage associated with an investment. Debt ratio, debt to equity, long term debt, short term debt and a host of others are used as business leverage barometers. You will see, the whole financial world wants to know that leverage is neutral; it just depends on how it is used.

It seems like nearly each time a client is advised to take profits on an investment that is at a high or purchase an investment that is not having a good year, they pause and ask, "Are you sure?" If a shirt that was normally $40.00 was on sale for $10.00 it seems reasonable that we would be excited with the discount. Yet with investments, we give pause to anything that is "on sale" and we want to hold tightly to something that has been profitable.

Go Shopping With The Rich!

Whoa, we're not going to Neiman Marcus* or Saks Fifth Avenue*! We are talking about opportunity here, opportunity to go shopping the same <u>way</u> rich folks do. If you think about all of the things you have bought and all of the things you have sold in your life, you probably have bought "better" than you have sold. In other words, most of us do a better job finding bargains on what we buy than we do making profits on what we sell. Why this happens is anybody's guess. Still, most folks I talk with also believe it's easier to buy low than sell high. Maybe we are better bargain shoppers than we are marketing specialists.

So, is it any surprise savvy investors find bargains...over and over. "The market **crashed**..." or "Do you think the market will recover?" "or is this time different?" "We may not pull out this time..." are just some of the popular woe-lines during bear (down) markets. Savvy investors listen to woe-lines as a signal to start bargain hunting. They buy on pessimism and sell on optimism, because they too believe it's easier to spot a bargain than it is to sell at a high price. We all know that timing the market as an individual is extremely difficult. And of course we all fear that what we buy today may be worth less tomorrow. But, if you have time to wait it out, why not buy low?

Sounds simple until you stand there trying to make a decision right? Try this. The next time you see the heralding of gloom and doom with some particular investment, ask yourself these questions. 1) Do I think that the USA is going out of business or close to it? 2) Do I believe that we will have some takeover of the USA that will cause us to lose all personal property? 3) Do I believe that this problem/fear/issue will remain with us for many, many years to come? If you answer "No" to these three questions, then opportunity may be knocking. Please understand that this does not account for timeframe, lost opportunity, the time value of money, or risk. But, the concept is still true. Buy on pessimism and sell on optimism. Can you think of a market or sector that is burning hot with prices going up, and up, a market that is full of optimism? If you can, buyer beware. It may be time to sell.

It takes raw guts to buy or sell when an investment strategy has dropped significantly in price. Of course, if you can't sleep at night because of your purchase, don't do it! However, if you have time and a strong stomach, I suggest you go shopping with the rich!

Counting the true cost of anything is so important in finance. Optimism, zeal, and over confidence can cloud our judgment on a large purchase, even if used as an investment. Our ability to "afford" something by the monthly payment may mask the TRUE cost of the item. So often we have a tendency to overlook what will actually come out of our checkbook over time. If we purchase a motorcycle, we have to consider maintenance, insurance, repairs, licenses, taxes and so forth, not just the purchase price. Consider the true cost of something like a puppy or a boat. Every lawn mower, bicycle, car, or almost any other purchase you ever make will eventually break and need repaired. The monthly payment is only one piece of the financial puzzle, so learn to count the true cost of whatever you may buy.

It's Real Money, You know

Not long ago I was talking to a couple of friends (whom I consider to be very intelligent). They were describing their strange experiences while buying a new car. Both of them said when they had gone in to purchase their new wheels, the salesperson kept asking "How much can you afford per month?" On separate endeavors, both of my friends inquired about the purchase price yet the salespeople kept returning to the monthly payment question. Only after several attempts were they able to focus on the purchase price of the vehicle. I believe that these two friends of mine are the exceptions. The salespersons likely ask about the payment because they know this is how they sell the merchandise to the general population, and this is what really counts with most buyers. The monthly expenditure makes the determination.

Hold on, if we ONLY look at the payment, and set the purchase price aside, we are then in a financial trap. Compounding this philosophy will cause us to quickly use all of our available income for payments. Obviously, payments are unavoidable in many situations but use them as the last resort (when purchasing non-income producing items.) *It's real money you know!*

The trap: Looking at the purchase price as a secondary concern behind the payment. Regardless of whether or not we can afford a particular payment, what really matters is the total price. It's real money you know! Someone has to pay the money back to the lender. Theoretically, we could afford to buy Manhattan at twice what it is worth if we could stretch the payment over enough years at a low enough interest rate.

So what is the fault in considering the payment without regard to the total price? The shopkeeper certainly comes out ahead, since this allows the merchandise to be sold at top dollar IF the payment is palatable to the buyer. The financing means everything! The payment could be most affordable, yet we could overpay for the item. Repeat the process on a home, a car, recreational vehicle, a lake house, a boat etc. Soon we, like so many will have whistled away our paycheck in payments. Now we are trapped. Ask anyone who writes loans, and I think they will quickly agree this happens constantly in American households. Have you ever known someone who still owed more on an item than its current value? It is often referred to as being "Upside-Down" Don't go there!, It is a very expensive endeavor.

The solution? Simple. Focus on the price, <u>not</u> the payment. Afford the price first, *then* hone the payment. When you commit to a payment, you commit to a purchase price, and the purchase price IS what you are paying. It IS what will come out of your bank account when you total all of those affordable payments. *It's real money you know!*

Periodically a client will discuss a potential real estate purchase as part of their portfolio. But, often it is at a time when the stock market has poor performance. It is always a discussion when the stock market has poor performance. It is common for a family to experiment with a rental duplex or a three family flat. There is money to be made in real estate or just about anything else, but real estate often requires active participation which makes it different than many investments. When the tenants say that the heat does not come on, then the landlord must meet the heating company at the site and determine the problem and the solution. They may discover something as simple as the tenant did not know how to operate the system. The afternoon is wasted, maybe for the third time this month. When the call comes on a major holiday or while you are on vacation, you may question your commitment to such an endeavor. Physical real estate, unlike some investments, must be "fed", even if there is no income. Taxes, insurance, and maintenance still have to be paid, even if the tenant is behind on their rent. Active participation can become another part time job. Real estate can require capital outlays in lean times. If you own active participation real estate it is worthwhile having a stockpile of cash for those times when your property needs fed.

Feeding the property becomes burdensome when the value decreases. Like any other investment, real estate values cycle. Yet, clients may claim that they are investing in real estate because "real estate never goes down…" In the recession of 2008/2009 that sentence was uttered by none, because real estate fell like a rock from the sky. Farm ground, antique autos, stocks, bonds, gold, and just about anything else go in and out of favor due to countless outside influences. Investments cycle, sometimes over long periods, sometimes quickly, but they cycle. Make sure you are ready to keep illiquid investments for a very long time.

Is The Real Estate Caution Light On?

*Fixing a leaky toilet will be a small problem compared to collecting the rent.

*"Is the Light On" was written before the recession of 2008, but it is still just as pertinent today.

Some would say yes; some would say no. You probably know people who hold firmly to each view. I have to admit I have more questions than answers within the real estate world, but with any market, it is important to learn some simple guidelines, and then apply them to the specific situation.

Guideline #1: Markets Change

Guideline #2: Most (non-obsolete) markets fluctuate or follow a cyclical pattern

Guideline #3: Markets often change suddenly

The first guideline says markets change. Opinions change, values change, and therefore, opportunities change. In America, the capitalist is free to move wherever they need to go in order to seize opportunity. If there is a shortage of anything in the USA, some entrepreneur will devise an alternative or figure out how to produce more. When supply exceeds demand, prices drop. What is popular now may change for many reasons including a simple media blitz (we call this headline risk). People like variety. Newer and better comes along. Products have life cycles, and so on. We want to remember that change is inevitable.

Guideline #2 tells us that if a market is not obsolete, outdated or severely out of favor, then it will most likely *cycle*. Take large automobiles for example. Remember the oil embargos? Large sedans quickly dropped in price as America became obsessed with "miles per gallon." Then a few years back, manufacturers began marketing the largest vehicles in years as fuel prices began to drop. My other favorite is the ceiling fan. The only ceiling fan I saw growing up was in the movie "Casablanca." Today nearly ever home on the block has several. The whole house fan was in nearly every house in the 1970s, yet today you might have trouble finding one on a shelf. Markets cycle.

Guideline #3, the rapid change of markets, is readily visible in the stock markets, technological markets, and any other fast-paced industry. For example, think about computers. Try selling your computer that you bought 5 years ago. I'll guess you will have very few interested buyers! Electronics is a fast moving industry.

So finally, we apply these guidelines to real estate. My caution light begins to glow whenever I see an industry or sector that continues to rise, rise, rise. Why you say? Because America is built on capitalism. Supply and demand will always pull together. Stay with me. Real Estate in St. Louis has prospered long enough that it is often viewed as a safe haven, but the rules apply to any region. Here are a few questions that come to mind when I see real estate burning very "hot".

- Is the real estate market experiencing an influx of cash as a result of a low stock market?

- Is the real estate supply going up, or will it go up in the near future? Conversely, is demand going down, or will it go down in the future?

- What factors are driving real estate prices up? Is this increase resulting from inflows of cash from a bearish stock market? Are low interest rates spurring first time home buyers to ownership?

- Is there a buying frenzy being fostered by good old-fashioned prosperity?

- Could a population shift such as an exodus of retirees from the work force expand the middle market as they "down-size"?

As you see I have more questions than answers, but I do believe that history will repeat. I hear everywhere euphoric statements of the generation of wealth through real estate and it is sounding hauntingly familiar to the conversations about the bountiful stock market in 1999. Look ahead into the future and make your bets on real estate. As for me…I'm turning on the "Caution" light.

CHAPTER 5

INVESTING, GAMBLING, AND SAVING

Don't Be A Saver!

I t is important to know who you are, how you process information and what causes worry in your life. It is important to determine if you are an investor, a gambler, a saver or a mixture of all three!

(PART I The Gatherers And The Planters)

I know plenty of folks who seem to already be living this "Don't Be A Saver" title, but what I really intend to say is, "Don't JUST be a saver." Why, you ask? Because it is extremely difficult to <u>save</u> your way to prosperity. Some people are savers, and some people are investors. Consider this analogy. Think of savers as gatherers of seeds and investors as farmers who plant and care for the seeds they have gathered.

Every farmer has to be a gatherer (of seed) but gatherers do not have to ever become farmers. I believe farmers are far more rare than gatherers, yet nearly *everyone says* they are a farmer. What's the difference in these two? Try these:

Some characteristics of a gatherer (saver):

- Needs to see the account go up every statement.

- Prefer safety over returns (They prefer having the seed in the silo as opposed to planting them and risking a bad crop)

- Does not care to stomach volatile markets

- Does not like risk. They are risk avoidant

- Enjoys watching the account grow (Filling the silo)

    Here are some characteristics of a farmer (investor):

- Willing to be a contrarian, or someone who will go against popular trends/wisdom

- Has time to wait, has patience. (Willing to sow in the spring and reap in the fall.)

- Is willing to spend the time necessary to learn about investing. (studies the crops)

- Does not get spooked easily, even from a bad financial experience (A failed crop.)

- Enjoys thinking about the payoff in the future. (The harvest).

- Often not conservative by nature, often enjoys the sport of the risk (Will it rain or not?)

So are you a gatherer or a planter? I find that nearly everyone *says* they are a farmer, but really many are gatherers at heart. There is nothing wrong with that, provided they understand the long term impact of *not farming*.

In part II we will look at the effects of gathering year after year.

Don't Be A Saver!
(PART II of The Gatherers And The Planters)

In Part I of this article we discussed how it is extremely difficult to save your way to prosperity. We said that many people are savers and many are investors, then we drew an analogy to gatherers and farmers, with savers being gatherers of seed and investors being planters of seed.

Consider this: interest income gets reported on your tax return and therefore is eroded quickly by taxes and inflation. A household that is in the 28% tax bracket will pay Federal income tax, State income tax (approximately 6%), and most likely FICA (approximately 7%). On the earned *income* if a thousand dollar bill were placed on simple interest for one year we might see:

Suppose 5% interest on $1000 =	$50.00
Less FICA/Fed tax/State Tax =	(20.50)
Inflation (on $1,000) =	(31.50)
	————
Profit/(Loss) Available to spend =	$(2.00)

Depending on where and how the money is used we could have sales tax on our purchase as well. Except those little brackets mean that we have not made any after tax money. We have LOST $2.00 because the inflation is figured on the original $1,000 seed money.

Now consider the same formula with a $10,000 bill using the same criteria:

Suppose 5% interest on $10,000=	$500
Less FICA/Fed tax/State Tax=	($205.00)
Inflation (on $10,000)=	($315.00)
	————
Profit/(Loss) Available to spend=	$(200.00)

<u>We lost more than we got to keep!</u> Do you see it? In our example, every year you only save at 5%*, you fall further and further behind. Now you understand the impact of taxes on saved money. You can plug in any amount of money and you will see that given these tax rates and this interest rate, a saver may lose purchasing power every year with taxes and inflation taken into account. I believe that if the average American understood our taxation, they would not be happy tax payers!

Now we understand why it is so difficult to save our way to prosperity. Knowing how the tax code reads now takes on new significance when we see what it does to our hard earned profits.

We all know of some little couple who saved every dime they ever made. This difficult path of the saver could possibly have made their lives easier if they would have understood the effects of taxes and inflation.

So how is the farmer any different you may ask. The farmer wants to earn <u>ABOVE</u> the inflation rate <u>AND</u> then a profit. The farmer battles the same inflation but realizes there must be a return over and above inflation for anyone to prosper and they are willing to accept the risk of loss to get that profit.

*Your interest could be more or less depending on interest rates.

Learning to Recognize An Investment

The word "investment" comes from the Latin word "investio" or our English version: "invest." My Webster Encyclopedic Dictionary tells me "investment" means four things:

1. To get dressed, or to clothe.

2. To besiege by military force.

3. The act of laying out money to purchase property. You've done this one too.

4. Spending money to hopefully make a profit.

I don't know about you, but I've never used any definition but the fourth, to spend money in anticipation of profit. I'll just bet that you are the same. So when someone says "I just made a big investment", they usually mean they purchased something that will return a profit right? Haven't you heard people say they are going to make an investment in a new car, yet have no intention of making a profit when it is sold? Conversely, we all know of cars that have become quite good investments for their owners. The same is true for certain pieces of real estate, certain Beanie Babies®, certain antiques, certain baseball cards, certain toys and so on. But I'll take this whole investment thing a step further. Nearly anything can be an investment, and nearly anything can become a liability. (I like to think of an investment as something that hopefully returns *more* than I put into it and a liability as something that returns *less* than I put into it or no return at all.)

So, how do you spot an investment? They come in all shapes, sizes, and price ranges. Sometimes a small investment can reap a substantial sum of money, and unfortunately sometimes someone's life savings is invested with every intent of a sizeable return only to find it worth little or nothing years later. Are those with the golden touch always lucky? I don't believe they are.

Few investments are without risk. Most can veer out of control sooner or later. When this happens, I believe the savvy investor does one of three things:

a) Sees it coming (long before the less experienced) and liquidates, or

b) has seen it before and is able to ride it out with patience, or

c) uses it as an opportunity to invest heavier.

Bottom line: I believe you can turn anything into gold. The trick is recognizing a good investment strategy and even more importantly, recognizing a lemon that's had the juice squeezed out of it! Usually the more information you have on the investment, the easier it is to make good decisions. Learn all you can about your favorite investment. Specialize a bit, study a single investment sector. America is full of books, articles, websites, videos and libraries on whatever you are interested in. Talk to one of those "lucky" investors that seem to know just what to buy and what not to buy. You might be surprised how they have stories of their initial failures in the same field that is now so "lucky". Start slow at first. Take your time and do the research. That big player you always hear about didn't start big. They have learned how to minimize risk and spend money to make a profit.

Trailing the Market

Often a client will say "I want to buy fund "X" or stock "Z". When asked why, they will say "Because, it has made twenty some percent so far this year." Or they will say, "My friend is in a fund that has gone up 17% in the last ten days, get me in too." Often they move into the fund or stock and see a few weeks or months of good returns. They are pleased with their decision but shortly thereafter they lose what they gained and actually dip below their original outlay. They decide to hang on until it goes back up. Finally, after several months they sell to cut their losses and start the cycle again. In the investment business we call these folks market timers or investors that trail the market. Let's side track a moment. Have you ever been in traffic and noticed that when a lane breaks free, several blinkers will come on and cars begin switching lanes? Within minutes, it seems all lanes are moving at the same pace again. What happened? The highway is an efficient place and folks react quickly to opportunity. Similarly, those mutual fund hunters or stock buyers will often put their blinkers on and change funds in a flash.

There have been thousands of articles written about market timing. This strategy simply does not work long term for the average investor, because it is quite emotional. There are volumes of studies that have been conducted to determine that it does not work. Yet, this seems to have little impact on those that continue to try.

When you get tempted to look at past returns to pick your next venture, just know that this is no guarantee of what will happen tomorrow and often we see the success drive inflows, which drives the price higher and higher, which in turn leads to a correction. Go look at one of your prospectuses and you will likely see "Past performance is no guarantee of future returns" displayed in several places. (Actually, contrarians would say that there is a greater chance that it will have a decrease because it has already gone up so much.) But now it appears we have painted ourselves into a corner. Past performance is the only data available, and it does give us some indication of the long term performance of the fund. But, it does not assure us performance in the future. The real trick is deciding what you <u>think</u> the fund will do next. In other words we want to try to be at the right place at the right time…on purpose! We want to educate ourselves so that we are positioned to ride the wave whenever it comes. There are countless philosophies on what does work in picking your next venture which is beyond the scope of this column. The point here is that timing the market does not work for individuals. (Even sophisticated computer algorithms have plenty of trouble.) If you are trying to "punch in, punch-out" of stocks, I believe eventually your financial boat will run ashore. If you hear of someone that claims they have been very successful with market timing you had better see their tax return before you put too much "stock" into what they say!

Instant Oats

Instant oats, Minute Rice*, microwave popcorn, buy now-pay later, instant oil change, quick-set, instant-on TV, and the list goes on. Sometimes we get in "lickety-split" mode. Often we want instant gratification...and we want it now. None of us like to wait. But instant usually costs money. Not so long ago I sat at my computer in frustration and exclaimed, "Why does it take so many seconds to transmit five million bytes of electronic information!" What am I saying? Well, if it is any consolation, other cultures have the same trouble with this "instant" idea.

A friend of mine is a Missionary. One of his biggest challenges in working with the local farmers is getting them to reject the idea of instant gratification. It works like this: For months they till the ground, remove the weeds, fertilize, plant and cultivate the plants. The harvest is good and everyone is delighted, except when he says They have to hold back some of the seeds for next year. Suddenly he is the ole "stick-in-the-mud." Why not sell the seed and enjoy the money...NOW? (Note that buying seed the next year is both difficult and expensive in their country.) The cost effective way to plant next year is to set aside an amount from this year's harvest. Although, it's not nearly as fun as selling all of the seed and getting a bigger paycheck <u>this</u> year.

Everyday I talk to Americans who spend every dime of every paycheck. Over time, they have allocated everything to a payment of some type or other. "Save some of each paycheck? Every week?" they say with raised eyebrows. "I don't have any extra!" "It's all spent." "Maybe when I get a better job."

In our instant society we grow accustomed to right-now satisfaction. But it has a really big price tag. Not getting the matching portion of that 401K or Simple IRA is money lost that will never be recaptured, and money that is a match can be a 100% return on day one in some plans. Likewise, waiting to contribute to your Roth IRA until next year means past year's allowable contributions are lost.

We recommend changing financial habits gradually. Start saving slowly. Try setting aside a little seed money from this week's paycheck. No matter how small, do it this week. Find a few dollars (seeds) to set aside. Have a garage sale, give up a dinner, give up a coffee, whatever. Get accustomed to only spending part of what you make. If you don't, the seasons will keep right on changing. You will have no seed to plant. The harvest will be small, and soon you will have become poor...but not instantly!

CHAPTER 6

Gaining Wealth Will Take Some Effort On Your Part

Gaining wealth will take effort on your part but often the effort is not nearly as significant as our imaginations might suggest. Any good habit starts with a reluctant first try, then another and then another. Right motivation follows right action. Gaining wealth is not some trick or magical DNA that someone inherits, but a way of thinking that develops over time. Wealth is obtainable as evidenced by so many that have started with nothing and prospered so greatly throughout their lives. Gaining wealth will not be without sacrifice and stamina, but never forget it is an obtainable goal on nearly any income level.

This chapter bears its title because in so many classes, and or lectures on finance I routinely see the person that is disappointed that they have not gleaned some "magic formula" that they could instantly use to triple their money in five minutes. When they discover that they will actually have effort on their part, they are sometimes content to remain in their old broken financial state. Building wealth takes effort and discipline, but it is not difficult. These principals are usually slow, mechanical and unexciting, but they have been proven over and over.

Perhaps people are so intrigued by the lottery because if you win, it replaces a lifetime of effort. The trouble is, when they win that large sum, they are still using the same financial principles that led them to NEED a lottery ticket in the first place. So if the same principles that led to hardship on a small scale are used on a larger scale, it seems reasonable to believe the larger scale mismanagement will simply create another mess, only this time it is a larger mess. So master the art of small increments.

You can water a newly planted tree by filling a five gallon bucket with water and putting the smallest hole in the bottom of the bucket and placing the bucket near the base of the tree. By the next morning the bucket will be completely empty and will have very slowly watered the tree. Now consider your financial life as the water in the bucket. The small holes in your budget amplify the same principal and drain your accounts slowly, but steadily. Now take a new bucket with no holes and allow the hose to drip into the top as slowly as you can make it drip. In a very short time the bucket will be full of water even though the drip was almost undetectable. This is the principal of wealth that we are discussing next.

Have you ever noticed how we have a tendency to avoid things we do not understand? How many teenagers neglect their algebra because it is a subject that takes a reasonable amount of effort to understand? As we get older, we trade algebra for taxes. Granted taxes CAN be harder to understand than some areas of finance, but they can be very powerful in changing your future outcome. So many people complain about the taxes they pay, yet pay more taxes than they are required to pay year after year simply because they do not take advantage of the opportunities the IRS allows them to take. Furthermore, we hear the phrase, "The rich get all of the (tax) breaks." While I have not seen much of that in my years in the business, if it is true, why not become rich and use it to your advantage. You cannot take advantage of tax breaks if you are unaware of the available tax breaks. If you have never bought a book about saving on taxes, perhaps this is an area you would like to explore. In any case, start by selling your trash.

Sell Your Trash

If you and I were neighbors and we were both walking down our driveways to take out the trash at the same time, we might strike-up a conversation. What would you say if I asked you to *sell* me some of what you are throwing away? Would you? Furthermore, what if I said *you* could select what you put in the bag that you sell? That's almost exactly what Uncle Sam says you can do.

Every year at tax time I ask, "Did you donate any clothing/furniture/ household items to The Salvation Army, Goodwill, or the American Veterans, a homeless shelter or a church benevolence program? Often the answer comes back, "No." "Nothing?" I ask.

They usually reply, "I really need to start doing that." You see, if you itemize schedule A of your Federal return you are allowed to deduct fair market value for clothing, furniture, toys, tools, stocks, bonds, jewelry, art or a multitude of items donated to charity.

Prosperity often produces waste and if we are not careful, we could be throwing away money. When the garage sale is over and there are two tables worth of treasures left over, box them and donate them. You will get a percentage of your donation back as raw cash from your tax return. As a rule of thumb you will get about a third of the value of the item back on your tax refund. Uncle Sam actually encourages you to donate to charities. For many people this can be hundreds or thousands of dollars. Be sure and document the value of your donated items with blue book pricing, E-Bay comparables, or some type of substantiation and keep that with your tax return detail. You will have to fill out one extra form if you exceed a certain threshold so be sure and document when you purchased the item, what it cost, when you donated it and so on.

Our tax code really allows for some flexibility when it comes to donations. For example, did you know that you can generally donate an item and deduct the *fair market value of the item, regardless of what it cost you*? Imagine if you donate an item that was worth $2,000 yet only cost you $100. Many non-profit organizations will accept your old car, tools, appliances, furniture, even old cell phones. So stop carrying everything to the street and start selling it back to the government. You won't even have to trouble yourself with the garage sale!

Keeping good records for tax time can really add up. Of course if you want to pay more taxes, the rest of us would like to thank you for your extra tax donation!

"Change"... Your Future

Not long ago I was engaged in casual conversation at a local fast food restaurant when I glanced at the floor and noticed a lonely nickel just lying there, right out in the open. A line of people shuffled by as they waited to place their orders. I'm sure some could not see that poor helpless nickel while others passed by, seemingly uninterested in it's fate. I made no effort at rescue. I became intrigued watching the outcome of the nickel. Just then an employee came by with broom and pan, and "swoosh." It was swept away with other assorted pieces of food and trash. "The employee is going to put that in his pocket," I thought. But I was wrong. He set the broom pan down and returned to the kitchen. Then my ten-year-old son, who had been watching the ordeal, said, "It's just a nickel, Dad."

He was right. It was just a nickel. However, his philosophy, like the fast food employee's, was that a nickel is worthless. I can't think of much you could buy with a nickel, but several nickels are a different story. Stay with me.

Every evening when I come home from work, I seem to have a pocket full of change. (Not from the floor though!) This change is the remnant of dollars used for coffee, lunch, gas, a pack of gum, a soda etc. At the end of the day, the change adds up. We always seem to have some on the dresser, in the seats and consoles of our cars, in our desks and so on.

Try throwing that change in a jar, or drawer or somewhere that you can watch it grow. Don't spend change at the store, make yourself use only paper bills for store purchases. This way every purchase causes you to save. If your bill is $3.02 use $4.00 and throw the $0.98 in that jar as a forced savings plan. If you assume three purchases a day with an average of $0.50 left from each purchase you would have $10.50 a week in savings. If there are two people in the family, then you save nearly $1,100 a year, IN CHANGE!

What a great way to save for next year's vacation! Start a vacation fund and ask all family members to toss in their change! Or use that pocket change as seed money for an investment, an individual retirement account, a birthday fund, a nice dinner out fund, or whatever else you can dream.

I have yet to meet a wealthy individual who says, "It's only a nickel." I'm sure they are out there, but as a general rule those who have millions also save nickels! One nickel doesn't make them wealthy, but their conservative philosophies do!

PS. I routinely see people at the grocery store using the counting machines for jars of change. I wonder what they do with the money?

Turning Miles Into Money

Every year at tax time, when we are preparing their return I ask clients about their mileage. Often I hear this answer "I should have written that down". In my opinion, they are correct, because the IRS forms ask if there is written record of mileage claims. No one enjoys paying for fuel, so keeping a mileage log in your car is a easy way to get a fat rebate on that fuel bill when you file your taxes. Here are a few of the miles that you might consider tracking:

Business Miles: If you drive your vehicle for your job, write down the miles for every trip. Sales people, plant managers, manufacturer representatives and managers of multiple locations have obvious mileage claims. But, if you have a mandatory off-site meeting or are required to go to another building or location during the day, record the mileage. You may be surprised how many you have. If you are not reimbursed by your company for any company travel, write it down!

Commuting Miles: I really wish we could claim a daily commute. Unfortunately that only works for miles driven from the first job to the second job.

Charity Miles: Many clients are surprised to discover that miles driven for not-for-profit charities may be claimed. The list of qualifying charities is endless. And while the credit amount differs from business, volunteering for a hospital or church may consume more fuel than you realize over a year's time. Relief work for disasters like hurricanes are also sometimes listed for special consideration at special rates.

Medical Miles: Medical miles are significant for some families during some years. If you have an immediate family member who requires hospital visits, doctor appointments, treatments, etc. write it down; you may exceed the threshold and be able to deduct.

To track mileage, get a little notebook or just a sheet of paper for the glove box in each car and note the following about each trip: date, purpose, start mileage, end mileage and destination. It does not take that long to jot down a couple of notes. I know some businessmen who keep spreadsheets on their phones.

Not sure which miles count and which do not? Write it down and sort them out at tax time. On your tax return, you will find that there is more than one way to claim those miles driven and you will also find that some mileage has a "floor" that you have to reach. For example some mileage has to exceed a certain percent of your adjusted gross income before you start receiving dollars back on that tax return. As always, consult your tax advisor for current information. The mileage rates published by the IRS changes sometimes even during the middle of a tax year but remember they are basing it only partially on fuel prices. It is so easy to get in the habit of reaching for your mileage log when you know it could translate into big dollars! Fortunately, they also give you credit for tires, oil, service etc. when they figure the mileage rates.

A home is one of if not the most expensive purchases the average family makes. And the older we get, the more distasteful the lingering mortgage seems to become. In short, most people feel more calm and secure when the house is paid off. In many household budgets, the mortgage is the single largest expenditure and without that one bill, it takes far less to live a comfortable life. Try making double payments.

Making Double Payments

Although our firm does not lend money, I quite often have clients ask about loans specifically home mortgages. These questions usually have to do with choices of 15-year payback periods, 30-year periods, and of course decisions over adjustable rate mortgages (ARMS) and traditional fixed products. Somewhere in the conversation I ask id they could make a double payment. Nearly every time I get a blank stare and find out they believe I mean <u>two entire house payments.</u> If you thought the same thing read on!

If you contact your current mortgage company and request an amortization schedule, they will send you a print-out that shows every payment that you must make to retire the debt on your home or property. Each payment will be listed and will be broken down into the principle portion and the interest portion. Chances are on your house you have a declining balance loan meaning you only pay interest on the unpaid balance. So the amount of interest will be different each month because the unpaid balance is different each month.

Here is the bottom line: to make a double payment, you pay the current month's principle and interest and the next month's principle portion. You SKIP next month's interest. Why? Because you paid this amount early and therefore did not have as large of a principle balance left on loan. For example, if we borrowed $100,000 at 7% our payment would be approximately $82.00 principle and $583.00 interest for the first payment of $665.00. The twelfth payment (one year later) is the same amount, $665.00, but the principle is $87.00 and the interest is $578.00. A double payment would be $87.00 principle $578.00 interest + $87.00 principle for the next month. Quickly we see that we could make triple payments for a total of $752.00. If we make double payments, our loan would be paid off in roughly ½ of the time. If we made triple payments, our 30-year note would be retired in 10 years, or 1/3 of the time.

Side note: Opponents of long mortgages would argue that 30-year mortgages have higher interest rates so they recommend choosing a 15-year note to get a lower interest rate. It is true that a 15-year loan will usually have a lower interest rate since the lender's risk period is shortened. But that 15-year note will also have a higher monthly payment. Always consider the risk. In hard times, a 30-year mortgage gives great peace of mind with its lower payment. If things are going well, that is wonderful. Make double payments or even more, because you understand how!

Chances are if you call your existing lender and ask them for that amortization schedule, they will send you one for no cost. Highlight each principle and each interest payment you make. Soon you will see just how easy it is to make extra principle payments and just how much interest you really can save.

So many companies have a savings plan for their employees. Yet so many employees fail to use this benefit. When prodded by our staff, employees that have access to a retirement plan will shrug their shoulders and respond with apathy to the free money offered to them, as if they were already independently wealthy. As of this writing we know of no mandate to give this money away, yet employers do so everyday to offer their employees a way to provide for the future. A "match" on a company plan is free and lucrative! It is a pay increase that lasts during your entire tenure. Why so many find no interest in this powerful tool will always be a mystery to me. Conquer this concept and you will have found a gem.

Free Money Please

Traditional IRAs, Roth IRAs, 401Ks, Money purchase plans, SEPS, profit sharing plans; Whew! The list seems endless. How do you determine which one is right for you? Save for the future, save for a loved-one's college, save for my heirs, for retirement. But how do I decide where to put the money? It may not be as difficult as you think. Here's one no-brainer!

Free money is hard to beat! If your employer has any kind of dollar matching program for which you are eligible, it is usually to your benefit to be enrolled. Why? Because it may be the only place you'll find free money. If you are offered a savings matching plan, take the money! Let me explain. They are giving you an incentive to continue employment with them. Try to put in the full amount for which they match. For example: if your employer matches dollar for dollar up to 3% of your saved amount, this means for each dollar you put into your retirement account, they will give you another dollar to match, up to 3% of your salary. So if you save 3% and they give you 3% (Free money!) you have saved 6%. As soon as the money is vested* you can take it with you should you leave the company. Be aware that the cap amount and the matching amount are not always the same. Check with your plan administrator. Many plans will allow you to borrow the funds, withdraw them for hardship, for college tuition or even a first time home purchase. Be sure you understand the details of your plan. Ask your administrator for the summary plan description which will clarify these details. Do you find it hard to deduct even the matched amount from your check? Start small. Increase as often as your plan will allow until you get up to the matched amount. I think someday you'll be glad you did!

There are a host of other ways to keep investing while making the tax laws work in your favor but that's for another time. Your tax advisor or investment representative is a good place to start the process.

Often companies require you to work a certain period of time before the money they contribute to your account is truly yours. Periods of one to five years are common on a pro-rated basis. After this period, the "matched" portion cannot be retained by the company should you terminate employment with them.

CHAPTER 7

THINKING LIKE THE RICH

The next article explains a powerful concept that is hard to begin but magical once mastered. It can change your financial picture and your quality of life.

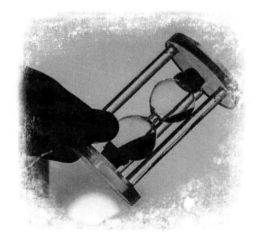

I Learned a lot From Dr. Not

I call him Dr. Not, because he dropped out of his <u>final</u> year of medical school! His parents were probably already bragging. It must have been bad grades, lack of funds, disillusionment or one of the other standard reasons for dropping out I thought. Wrong! This is what he told me, "I can't sell my time, because there isn't enough to sell." I was confused, but he went on to explain that he decided since he only had 24 possible hours each day, and since he reserved eight of those for sleeping, he just couldn't afford to sell many more. He said, "Thankfully, I realized before it was too late, that for me to make money I had to spend time seeing patients!" Dr. Not had a point. To earn an income, he would have to see patients, and lots of them. Instead, he wanted to be in a business that could make money even while he was NOT spending time on it. He wanted to be in a business that wasn't compensating him based on how much of his time he sold. So in his last year of medical school he dropped out and started a company of his own.

I found a real jewel in his advice and have always remembered the lesson. We all want a way to make money without active involvement. Sometimes we have no choice, we have to sell our time because that's the way our job pays. Certainly many folks are quite happy selling their time and wouldn't have it any other way. No problem. But for those who agree with Dr. Not, when the job changes, opportunity knocks, or when you just plain get tired of selling your time, look for a position where you can make money with your *ability* rather than your time. How often we look at just the pay and skip the rest. Not long ago I was offered a position that more than doubled my present salary. The environment was great, the people were super and the benefits were ones we all covet. Except, they really wanted to purchase my time...all of it! Not for sale. I declined. My time is just like yours....valuable, especially to me. I can't make more time. I can't stop it, stretch it, or change it. We all get 24 hours each day.

I heard about a very wise fella who was being questioned in a final interview about what office hours he would keep if he were given the job. He wisely replied, "Let's just say I'll get the job done." He got the position, and he gets the job done.

What about you? Are you making money while you are doing something else? What are you investing in?

PS. Today Dr. Not is the CEO of his own multimillion dollar industry giant. A smart investment. The best part is, just as he predicted, he now makes money without selling his time.

Someone once said, "Take your time, develop a plan and stick to the plan you develop." Sometimes in desperation or greed one can be tempted to stretch the rules. We are not building in this chapter. Creating, using and distributing wealth is quite enjoyable once you understand the principals. Some will even say it's easy. The first chair violinist makes you want to play a violin because he/she makes it look so easy. But when you pick up that bow for the first time, it is awkward at best. It feels like you have your pants on backwards. That violinist did not learn to play yesterday. You are witnessing years of honing a skill, and if you want to master anything, there is seldom a shortcut worth taking.

One Difference in the Wealthy and the Not-So-Wealthy!

Ask an accountant, a financial advisor or a tax professional to look at someone (whom they don't know) and tell you if that someone is rich or poor. I think they might all three give you the same answer: You can't tell by looking.

For example, we have all heard stories of the wealthy land barons that couldn't spend their interest, yet live like Mr. and Mrs. Average. Or, the owner of the multi-million dollar corporation that still drives an old dented pick-up truck. Even more puzzling are the folks next door who have average paying jobs yet already have next year's model sports car in the drive, display the latest fashion every time they leave the house and already own everything you want! Without studying their tax returns, I have found it difficult to tell who is wealthy and who is not! What I have learned is that the wealthy and the not-so-wealthy I know, certainly do NOT act or think the same when it comes to money.

I see some patterns. Often when those who are on shaky financial ground see something they want, they buy it. The end. However, when we buy something we can't afford on a regular basis, we must borrow more and more. Some folks go on this way for years. We don't need a course in finance to tell us that if we continually spend more than we make, eventually that habit will catch up with us.

Conversely, I find that financially savvy people live <u>below</u> their means. The ones I know seldom drive what they could afford to drive, seldom live where they could afford to live, and so on. These people <u>think</u> differently and therefore act differently. They routinely spend less than they can afford. Also, I find that they take purchases seriously. They ask questions like "Is it right for my situation?", "If I will eventually have to sell it, what value will it have?", "What will the maintenance costs be?", or "Should I spend more on higher quality or would one with lesser quality do?" Sometimes I see very wealthy people carefully consider what may appear to be a relatively small financial decision. So are they wealthy because they live this way or do they live this way because they are wealthy? Who cares, it works!

One difference in the wealthy and the not-so-wealthy…is how they think!

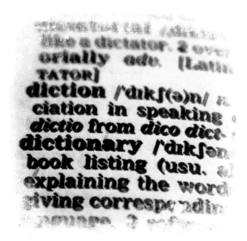

The Rich Use Different Definitions

Ask someone you know how they define an asset. Then, ask them to define a liability. (I have great fun with this when I speak to high school students.) The most common answer I get goes like this: "An asset is something that has value while a liability comes in the form of a bill." Under this definition a travel trailer (that is paid for) would be an asset because you own it free and clear, but your house would be a liability because you still have a mortgage that is due. Using the same definitions the high school students would use our asset/liability list would look like this:

Assets:	Liabilities:
Computer	Car
Personal Residence	Phone
Jewelry	Water Bill
Stereo/TV	Electric Bill
Rental house	
Antique automobile	
Stocks & Bonds	

So in the list above, the assets have value, the liabilities are really bills. Once upon a time, I believed the same way. However, I now know that the rich use different definitions for assets and liabilities.

Robert Kiyosaki in his book <u>Rich Dad Poor Dad</u> says, "Rich people acquire assets. The poor and middle class acquire liabilities, but they think they are assets". So he recommends we use different definitions.

Try defining an asset as something that *pays* you money. Try defining a liability as something that *costs* you money. With this new perspective the same list becomes:

Assets:	Liabilities:
Rental house	Car
Stocks & Bonds	Personal Residence
	Phone
	Jewelry
	Water Bill
	Stereo/TV
	Electric Bill
	Computer
	Antique automobile

Do you see what happened? Under the new definition, the liabilities column grew! Liabilities cost you money! The obvious example is your house. Is it an asset? No, because it does not make you money. It can have a mortgage, maintenance, heating, cooling bills, repairs and so on. The house really costs you money whereas the stocks, bonds and the rental house may generate income.

Wealthy people collect assets. Following through with their definition they then use income from their assets to purchase liabilities that they want.

As long as the asset column brings in more money than the liabilities column consumes, they don't have to work!

Try using these new asset/liability definitions during the next month. If you are like many Americans, you may find out that you are really a collector of liabilities, so something must change!

Shopping Skills!

The sign may say, "on sale", "one day only", "price reduction", while supplies last and so on. The vendor is reducing the price to sell the merchandise more quickly. I think most of us really enjoy a bargain, especially on an item that we know we have to buy anyway.

The next time we see some bargains, we might go on a large shopping spree. However, this time let's go shopping the same way the rich do. I don't mean we will be taking a limousine or a jet to a ritzy mall. Rather, we will stick close to home to do our shopping, with the same guidelines the rich use. Does this sound like fun?

Try these steps to sharpen your shopping skills: (1) Buy when the values are plentiful. (Do you leave the store with something every time, or are you selective?) This means we DO NOT buy just because we want to buy. Rather we buy when the value is apparent and plentiful. We all want to buy low and sell high, but both take a great amount of courage. If the price is very low, it may be because no one else is buying. If the price is very high, folks have a tendency not to sell. Perhaps the mindset is that the value will continue to rise still more. A contrarian would buy when the public is pessimistic about an item and sell when most folks are optimistic. (2) Purchase "out of season". If you are buying a barn, purchase in the winter when no one buys barns. Want a 4-wheel drive? Auto salesmen tell me they are cheaper in the spring (after the snow). Do you want real estate? Consider buying when the job market is slow, during a recession or when there is some stimulus that makes it unattractive.. So you are looking for bonds? They usually correlate with interest rates. They are "on sale" when interest rates are HIGH and are usually selling for a premium when interest rates are LOW. (3) Go searching for bargains. I've often heard people say "I never find deals like that." Deals usually have to be found, they don't ring your doorbell! Can't seem to find any bargains? Just keep looking. Persistence usually produces results.

One final note: Usually the reward for bearing some risk is reaped somewhere in the future. In other words, can you afford to remain in the game long enough to reap the rewards?

The Mystery of Success, Luck, And Good Fortune.

Mystery Story #1: I love to watch people buy lottery tickets at the gas station. Some will kiss the ticket, some will hold it as to say a little prayer, but most will guard it and keep it close until they are safe in their car, knowing it has to be a winner. They will warn, "You can't win if you don't play." (Yeah, bu you also can't lose if you don't play.) Have you ever listened to a winner on a television game show or the winner of a local raffle? Often they will say, "I have never won anything before." Count up the number of drawings, raffles, door prizes you have won in your life. The odds would say you have certainly lost far more often than you have won.

Mystery Story #2: Recently my wife and children were standing in the checkout line at a local store. As they glanced at the floor, there was a penny that my daughter was going to pick up and pocket. Just then the lady in line behind them warned, "No! Only pick up pennies that are facing heads-up. If they are facing tails-up, that's bad luck, let them be." A penny spends the same regardless of which way it falls. My daughter (age 9) knew to pick up the penny anyway. I wonder if this would this woman would give the same advice if she found a $100.00 bill facing tails-up?

Mystery Story #3: "How did you pick your stocks?" I'll ask. "Did you use fundamental analysis, technical analysis, a combination of the two?" The reply will often be that they picked the companies that they liked, or that company has a product that they like and (inferring that if they like the product then everyone must like the product.)

In my opinion all three of these stories have a common theme. The mystery of success, luck, and good fortune may be a mystery to these people because they may *be unaware they are simply playing the odds of chance*. If they do not win, they may feel unlucky. But really they are one more data point within the framework of the odds of winning and losing. What these folks call luck the mathematician would simply call probabilities and statistics. A statistician could tell them exactly what their chances of good fortune are with accuracy to nine decimal places!

Outside the area of money, we seldom would employ such behavior. For example, we do not take our "lucky streets" or a random path to get to work, we take the shortest/easiest route. We do not choose a spouse by lottery. If we needed heart surgery, would we look at a list of heart surgeons and pick the last name that sounded best? There are legitimate exceptions to every rule, but our approach to finances often seems to have an air of superstition applied that we use nowhere else in life. I heard a very successful man say once, the more I learn, the "luckier" I seem to become! America has great storehouses of information. Why not use this information to unravel the mystery of success, luck, and good fortune, and put the odds in your favor?

CHAPTER 8

THE NUTS AND BOLTS OF PRACTICAL FINANCE

Who Cares About Dividends?

If you have a walnut tree in your yard, it will drop walnuts, which are the dividends of walnut trees. Cherry trees give cherries as their dividends. Dividend funds give dollars!

You and I care, because dividends are money paid to the holders of the shares! All too often the boring pace of dividends gets lost in the noise from those who are searching for new, lucrative companies with soaring stock prices. You probably have been a part of conversations at the lunchroom table where an individual freely touts their market successes. I have heard it said, *"Never confuse brains and a bull market."* In other words, sometimes you can throw a dart at the <u>Wall Street</u> <u>Journal</u> and hit a stock or fund that is rising in price. Perhaps it took no intellect what-so-ever.

Conversely, when was the last time you heard lunch table talk about dividends? Probably never, right? When markets are blasting upward, even company management seems to pay less attention to dividends. I believe the reason for this shift in management thinking is that high profits eclipse a small dividend, (Not to mention the fact that dividends are really a distribution of profits so they are not a pre-tax deduction for the corporation.) But what about those markets where the general trend is downward? I care about dividends! *Never forget that dividends are hard evidence that profits actually exist.* If you have no profit, you certainly cannot have a distribution of profit (a dividend).

Do you remember the Popeye cartoons? Wimpy was one of the characters that Popeye interacted with regularly. And Wimpy used to say, "I'll gladly pay you on Tuesday for a hamburger today." (Obviously, Wimpy was living beyond his means!) Without a distribution of profits or a dividend, management is asking the shareholders for permission to pay later. They are asking to be trusted to return a higher stock price in the future.

Dividends are important because they are real money. But just to put the finishing touch on our discussion, consider this definition: Income + Growth = Return. It is fair for us to say income and growth both contribute to the total return and that dividends are income. An account with only growth potential relies solely on growth potential for gain. An account that has only income potential relies only on income potential for gain. Accounts with BOTH income and growth potential have two ways to return gain.

Think long and hard about dividends. Maybe you want to plant a dividend tree! They are small, slow and unexciting. But over time, they add up!

Purchasing power is critical when analyzing the time value of money. If you consider the price of a Ford Mustang today and the price of a Ford Mustang in 1967 you will find they are very, very different. The newer Mustang is multiples of the 1967 versions and that is partly due to the slow rising of prices over the last decades. If you buried your savings for a Mustang in 1967 and dug it up today, you would be far short of the purchase price, because the prices of things have risen. Gasoline was once twelve cents a gallon, a loaf of bread was once a quarter and a new Ford Mustang was at one time about twenty-five hundred dollars. Inflation is important in planning because it accounts for the increasing price of everyday items.

Finance Books Call It TVM

Finance books call it the time value of money (TVM), but few people beyond the author and students seem to care. However, the principle behind it is priceless to us all. If you are going to make money you have to understand it.

When you were a child, how much did a gallon of milk cost? Compare that to the price of milk today. I used one of the many inflation calculators on the internet and ran an interesting calculation. An item that cost $1,000 dollars today only cost $484.68 twenty years earlier. Why? Because of inflation. Inflation is the word financial types use to describe the erosion of your purchasing power due to the continual increase in prices. What cost $484.68 in 1981 is over twice as expensive just 20 years later, by 2001 and this is typical for many periods in history. This inflation keeps goods and services going up, up, up. And that $1,000 item in 2001, will cost even more in the future. The time value of money (TVM) is what we use to estimate what our purchasing power will be at any given time in the future.

Now, how do we use this information to our benefit? Let's use an example: A client comes in and wants a guaranteed interest rate on their investment. They can accomplish this with a fixed-interest rate product. I then remind them about the time value of money. If that client "fixed" the interest rate for one year at 4%, and inflation were at 3%, then at the end of the year they only made 4%-3% = 1%. And they have to pay taxes on the 4%! Ouch. We use a TVM calculation (on a special calculator) to see the effect of repeating this process over and over. Slowly, inflation erodes your purchasing power. This inflation has dwindled your money. In Brazil during unusually high inflationary times, I saw wine bibbers sleeping on the streets with money blowing up against them as they slept. Why? Because three grocery bags of money would not buy a stick of gum in Brazil during that high inflationary period. (This is quite unusual, but also shows you what can happen.) If you checked out of your hotel in the morning you only exchanged enough money for the day. At the end of the day, you threw away all currency you had left over because the day's inflation had eroded the value of the currency by the end of the day. This is an extreme case, but you get the point.

Three percent is used as a rule of thumb for yearly inflation increases. No matter how much you make, inflation will take it's toll. So you got a 3% raise this year? Not really, because inflation took the first 3%! What's the bottom line? We have to devise ways to average a rate of return that is higher than the rate of inflation. Anything less…well, we are getting poorer!

*Source: S. Morgan Friedman Calculator based upon Consumer Price Index statistics from Historical Statistics of the United States and annual Statistical Abstracts of the United States.

One of the benefits of remaining in a particular field of concentration for decades is that you find after a while, the trends start repeating. Interest rates are one of those financial topics that cycle. We all watch banks and interest rates to some degree. They are important if we are borrowing and if we are lending. Many have made a career understanding interest rates.

Benefit From Interest Rates...Regardless

When interest rates are low, we are all excited about the buying power that it affords us. Cars can be purchased at very low interest rates. Suddenly, you can afford a bigger house, a second house, or even THE dream house. Money is cheap in low interest rate environments. Prices may continue to rise, but you can still afford so much more than you ever thought possible. After all, you are paying very little interest on borrowed money. You may ask, "...and the down side?" The down side is that month after month your savings account does not increase. Your certificates of deposit (CDs) renew at lower and lower rates. You start hearing talk of people pulling their money out of the bank and stuffing it in their mattress or looking for more unusual and alternative investments.

When interest rates soar, the reverse happens. We can get very accustomed to nice performances on the savings account, CDs and just about every other fixed interest rate bearing investment. The down side is you can only afford a fraction of the house you could in a low interest rate environment. Cars become expensive, prices rise fast, and oh yes, that money that was stuffed in the mattress? It's gone. Gone to the bank and put on interest, every last dime! Who would pass up a great interest rate?

So the real question we all want answered is when do we have the best of both worlds? That is, low interest rates for money we borrow and high interest rates on our investments? In other words when can we have our cake and eat it too? The answer is NEVER. Not in a capitalistic society anyway.

Understand that lenders work off of the "spread." They buy money at a wholesale rate and sell it at a retail rate. For example: if you borrow money at prime (the preferred interest rate benchmark for businesses), then savings accounts must pay less than prime. If Prime were 6%, and your savings account were paying 4%, then the bank or lender gets to keep the spread of 2% (6%-4%=2%). The lender can still make 2% if prime were at 19% and savings accounts paid 17%.

How do we benefit from either situation? When interest rates are low, especially historic lows, you may want to borrow for the long term (if you need to borrow.) I see people using one year adjustable rate mortgages in historic low interest rate environments and ask, "Why?" Lock in your mortgage for 30 years and do just the opposite with your money that is invested. Commit to very short (1 year) terms on your CDs, annuities and any fixed interest rate accounts. And consider selling bonds. Then when interest rates rise, lock in your CDs, annuities and any fixed interest rate accounts for the long term, and consider buying bonds. Just a side note on bonds, usually when interest rates rise, bond prices decline and when interest rates fall, bond prices rise. This is as close to a "rule" in finance as you get. Financial environments always change, and you may benefit from interest rates, regardless of which way they move.

When Markets Become Worried

Nearly everyone has access to some very popular financial news channels on their television. They have pretty colors, the anchors are always dressed nice, are generally attractive and speak well, and many of the commercials are quite clever. Some call it financial entertainment. If the Dow Jones Industrial Average (DJIA) drops by 250 points, it's called a "plunge." If it goes up by 250 points, it "soared," even if that is only a 3% change. With that same logic an elevator on a 30 story building would "plunge" down one floor (3%) or "soar" up one floor (3%). It's no secret that "dull" is not an attention getter... especially on television*.

I believe financial markets are driven by two primary emotions: greed and fear. Similarly we have expressions that describe both. They are the common bull and bear markets. (Remember that bulls fight by jabbing their horns in an upward motion, while bears fight by slapping their paws downward. Hence, a bull market is an upward movement and a bear market is a downward trend.) In bull markets the sky is the limit, everyone wants on board, a little greed might appear in, and up, up, up we go. But what happens when markets become worried? The bear sets in (hibernates in some cases!) and down, down, down we go. Of course events like those of 9/11, wars, rumors of wars, forecasts, earnings reports, elections, natural disasters of all types, interest rate changes and such all contribute to market direction as well. But, these are the fuel for emotion. When markets become worried, we see a downward spiral. Leaders worry that worse will worsen! Down we go. The investor has become a worrier. The long term investor now watches hourly in anticipation of up signs or down signs. Investment plans are tossed in an instant. We start making a list of all the things we could have bought with the money that's gone. Fear has set in. "Should I go to cash?" "What do you think of Gold or precious metals?" "Tell me when to panic!" It is funny to us in the office when we receive very similar calls in close proximity from three different clients who all ask the same thing. By the third call we ask, "Have you been watching television?"

I often tell clients that our bodies are not designed to worry well. Medical science underlines this fact. We don't endorse sticking your head in the sand, but especially for people that are not using their investments as their only income stream, stop worrying and start living. Markets change, you could say that waves are a normal part of an ocean. If the change makes you miserable, consider being a saver instead. If you can bear the market (catch the pun!), stick to that boring, mechanical plan, and continue adding to your account on a regular basis. This worried bear will not last forever, and markets have a way of rewarding the brave.

PS. Next time you hear someone talk about the good ole days, ask them if they want to go back. You'll get a sharp, "No." The good ole days are now. If we have the basic necessities of life, why not enjoy them? Some of the best things in life are free anyway. Get to know your neighbors, enjoy family, go outdoors, eat ice cream, take a weekend get-away, talk to a child, paint, draw, learn to play a musical instrument. Stop worrying and start living. Markets never stay the same. Markets become worried, and when they do you are wise to take note, but stick to your financial plan! Five years from now today will be long forgotten.

* I am using satire here when we speak of financial news. I certainly believe there is great benefit in being informed and current.

If You Own Bonds, You Had Better Understand…Bonds.

As part of nearly every portfolio review we commence a discussion on the bond-equity mix of the account. The mix of these two portfolio players are so very important for a well diversified account. But we find sometimes the equities stocks are more understood than the bonds. Like equities, the bonds may be held in a fund, or individually but either way, they are still bonds.

Not every portfolio has a significant bond allocation, but if you own them individually, or have a fund that owns them, it might not be a bad idea to understand how they work. I find many clients understand <u>one </u>part of the bond very well, the <u>interest payment</u>, but pay little attention to the price of the bond.

There are two components to a bond: the interest payment and the selling price. The interest payment will come at some regular interval and will be a percentage of the bond. If a $10,000 bond pays 7%, then the interest would be $700 per year. Often unscrupulous brokers will sell bonds on interest rate without mentioning if the bond is at a discount or premium. The second component, the selling price of the bond, correlates to interest rates and can fluctuate a great deal. If sold this can add to or take away from that interest that is being earned.

Think of a see-saw when you were a child. Imagine that on one side of the see-saw is interest rates and the other side is bond (selling) prices. As interest rates go down, bond prices go up. As interest rates go up, bond prices go down. This is called an inverse (see-saw) relationship. This inverse relationship is not true of every bond or every fund, there are many exceptions. But in general, this is the idea. "So what?" you say. The "so what" is this: when a seventy-five year old client wants to purchase a bond that matures in thirty years (when they are 105 years old!) it is time to understand this inverse relationship! (Note that a 30-year bond could be worth far less than the par value or the face value if it is sold before 30 years.)

109

Now let's look for a little application. Think of the current economic environment, whatever it may be. Are interest rates generally high, low, or fairly average? If interest rates are very low, then bond selling prices will likely be adversely affected when interest rates rise. If interest rates are high right now then bonds will likely be selling at a discount. Not too tough right?

For those who elect not to watch so closely, there are blend funds which usually allow the fund managers to decide how many bonds of a certain type to hold at any given time. If interest rates are low, look up a few blend funds. You will probably see that the fund manager has bailed-out of his bonds and had a little profit taking, which may indicate that he believes interest rates will soon rise. So if it is bonds that you seek, remember to look at BOTH components of the bond: the interest rate and the selling price.

PS. The longer the term of the bond (like 30 year) the more closely it will correspond to this see-saw guideline. And of course the shorter the bonding maturity, the less affected it will be by this guideline. And remember: bonds sell at the par or face value at maturity.

Have you noticed that it is easier to complain about taxes than to implement a tax savings strategy? Eventually not making a decision to address future taxes will turn into a decision to pay MORE taxes! This concept just makes sense and can be a very powerful estate planning tool.

If You Want To Pay More Taxes, Ignore This.

I talk with folks nearly every week that sincerely desire to make good financial decisions concerning their retirement, yet look at me as if I'm from another world when I say "Why are you not using the government's TAX-FREE savings plan?" I often get a blank stare back. It seems that everyone has heard of a Roth Individual Retirement Account (IRA), yet many still believe it is too good to be true. I have to admit, I have had so many people question this tool, that I have even started doubting it myself, on occasion. When you withdraw money from a Roth IRA, IT IS TAX FREE. This is a huge gift from the government to you, but only if you use it. We could spend days covering all of the fine print of the Roth IRA but the government has already done that at www.irs.gov. Here are the quick highlights:

- Contributions to Roths are limited by the government. (Otherwise there would be no tax revenue to run the government in the future). If you make too much money from wages you will not get the full advantage, or are ineligible completely.

- A non-employed spouse can contribute to a Roth even though they do not have earned income.

- A minor can contribute if they have earned income.

- Unlike traditional (regular) IRAs, you get NO deduction for a Roth.

- Earnings are tax free.

- Contributions to a Roth are allowed even when the taxpayer is over 70 ½ years old.

- You can still contribute to a Roth even though you participate in an employer qualified retirement plan.

- Contributions can be made up through the due date of the tax return (no extensions.)

- Earnings are tax free! Did I mention that? Wow! (Look around the room you are in and name three things that were tax free!) You cannot find them.

- Original contributions can be withdrawn anytime. This is because the money came from your bank account and was not taken out of your paycheck before taxes.

When you withdraw money from a Roth IRA, it is tax free!

So potentially, the longer time horizon you have for this money to grow inside a Roth IRA, the greater this advantage could be. Please understand that "deferred tax" and "tax-free" are very, very different. Deferred is just what it says, deferred. You will pay the tax eventually. Tax free means free of tax. Death is inevitable, taxes are not (at least with a Roth IRA)! What are you waiting for?

P.S. If you inherit a Roth IRA, different rules apply.

Minors Can Have Roth IRAs!

Sometimes when I teach interns about finance I ask them this question: "What do you have that I want more of, but you cannot give me?" After some funny looks, someone will answer, "Time." "Absolutely, yes," I say. Then I explain that time is one of the basic ingredients for a wealth generation recipe. Compounding works over time; more time, more compounding, less time, less compounding. So, the sooner we start, obviously, the more time we have… for compounding! Now make the jump with me. Since the younger we are (or our children are) the more time there is for compounding and the more valuable tax free legislation becomes. A minor has a lot of time! But knowing how to capitalize on all of that time is part of the secret.

Since Roth IRA gains are meant to be a tax free tool, anyone with time, will find these especially valuable. Minors can have Roths! It's all about compounding over time!

So you can help your 15 year old along to becoming a millionaire if you can help him get some sort of income from a job. (Earned income is necessary to fund a Roth IRA.) Those who understand the tax law have no problem thinking about retirement when their children are 15 years old. I know one family that allows their son to work at the family business (within the framework of child labor laws*), mowing and cleaning in exchange for retirement income. The income can be used to fund a tax-free Roth IRA. Wow! Make sure they actually do the work, because funding a child's Roth to dilute company profits is NOT recommended.

Remember a child can put away thousands each year and can still withdraw the principal in the future for expenses including college, a first time home purchase etc. This child may not be too excited about forgoing another gadget, but they will likely be grateful for the early compounding boost, not to mention the tax free advantages that are very friendly to long term investors.

Owning a business is a clever way to use family members for supplemental work but it is *not* a requirement. Know that while not every investment sponsor will accept minor Roths, but there are certainly those that will.

* Check your state's homepage under the business or labor sections.

My Fund Went Down Yet I Still Owe Taxes?

Yes, it is called capital gains distributions. Every year at tax time I get a few of these questions, usually with a little grumpy tone thrown in.

What are capital gains distributions anyway? Review first: mutual funds are intended to provide diversification. Mutual funds that invest in stocks can make profits through the buying and selling of individual stocks. When an investor owns a share of a mutual fund, they are really mutually owning a small piece of many individual stocks. Because a mutual fund sells stock "X" there is either a gain or a loss. If there are more gains than losses, the fund is usually profitable. Where does this profit go? It goes back to the mutual owners of the mutual fund, of course, since they bore the risk with their money. Because profits are taxed by the government, and these profits go to the investors, so do the taxes. No such thing as a free lunch.

We have all kind of accepted taxation on profits and have become accustomed to paying Uncle Sam for our gains, but what about paying Uncle Sam when we lose? This gets investors a little more razzed at tax time. Here is what happens. Assume that on January 1st the fund was worth $50.00 per share, yet on December 31st of the same year the fund was worth $35.00 per share. Can there be a capital gain? You bet there can be a capital gain. The "why" has to do with stocks that were sold at a profit during the calendar year. Had they not, the fund price would be even lower. So even though the overall price of the mutual fund declined, there could have been very hefty profits on certain liquidations. You pay Uncle Sam when you profit, so of course distributions of interest and dividends are also going to contribute to the tax bill.

So when tax time comes around and you get your capital gains distribution statements you will understand why you are being taxed. It is not a fun bill to pay, but for many investors the taxes are a small price for making long term profits.

There are some advantages of exchange traded funds in the area of taxation, but we will have that for another time.

It seems that clients never volunteer the information that they have physical stock certificates at home. Perhaps it is an after thought, or maybe it is a secret nest egg, or some other reason. More often than not a financial advisor has to pry this information from a client. When the client understands this article, they cannot wait to take action.

Stock Certificates In The Lock Box

Money is a funny thing with lots of folks. Some who we think are dirt poor, may be very, very rich; and those who we think are very, very rich, may be a dollar from bankruptcy. Either way, it seems like we are all just a little skittish about broadcasting what we have…or don't have. Stock certificates are no exception. But the financial types usually ask. In fact, they have a duty to ask. And so somewhere along the way I say, "Do you have any stock certificates lying around?" If the answer comes back "Yes," then I explain this:

While you are breathing, and know who the President is, what year it is, your name, etc. it is fairly simple to transfer the stock certificates in the lock box to a brokerage account or book entry. A brokerage account is conveniently designed to help handle your beneficiary instructions, transfer instructions, dividend instructions, and so on. If you are the owner of such a certificate, your heirs will be grateful for such a move on your part. If you are the beneficiary of such a stock, you will be ecstatic that this was addressed while the owner was alive, especially when you read the next paragraph!

If something happens to the owner of that stock certificate before such a transfer has taken place, the plot thickens. Oh boy, does it thicken. In many cases the process is exceedingly long, complicated, frustrating and expensive. After all, the owner is no longer around to ask if this is a legitimate transfer or not. Precautions have to be taken. Letters of instruction, new account forms, original raised seal death certificates (not copies), affidavits of domicile, notary seals, signature guarantees, stock powers and so forth are usually necessary to take possession of the stock, even when it is clear that the legitimate beneficiary IS the one asking. Furthermore, the trustee <u>of each</u> company must be contacted via mail and will deliver specific instructions on how each of the stock certificate is to be processed. They may require additional documentation as well. Sound expensive? Good guess.

Sometimes we see sad cases where the sale of the stock would be very appropriate for paying estate taxes, funeral expenses or other estate matters, yet the family cannot get access because the stocks were in certificate form in a lockbox that no one knew existed. A year later, they are still bewildered by the complexity of it all. How do you top that? If the owner becomes incompetent in any way prior to death, another layer of complexity is introduced with durable power of attorney requirements.

So, take an hour now and save your loved ones a year of frustration. If you (or a family member) has stock certificates, you may want to consider a brokerage account to hold those stocks in book entry form.

The Star of Diversification

There are five point stars, movie stars, the Star of David, rock stars, shining stars, superstars, and even twinkle, twinkle, little stars. In your household finance we want you to look at the five point star, the star of diversification. Hold that thought. We routinely hear about the need to diversify *within* our portfolio. However, we seldom hear about diversity on a household level. For example, if I ask a client what kind of investments they have they will usually name one segment such as the stock market, certificates of deposit or even their house. Often folks have 95% of their wealth in one asset. They are quite possibly unbalanced in their investment approach. Now back to the star.

Try this at home, draw a regular five point star and at the end of each point, write one of your investment vehicles. As an example: Point 1: Antiques; Point 2: Stocks and bonds; Point 3: A family business; Point 4: Real estate. Point 5: Fixed interest bearing products. If you have only one or two points filled, your "all-star" may turn out to leave you lacking, as you have little margin for error. And the reason for needing several points? Simple. No-one knows the future. While we may have educated guesses, they are still only our best guess at what we believe will prove profitable in the future. If one point of our star completely dried up, we still have the other four to mitigate our risk. Even if we have all five points identified, it requires a constant watch to keep a *balanced* star. Note that we certainly may have a different percentage of our household portfolio weighted on each point. But as values rise and fall, we try to re-balance periodically.

Remember that client that said their house was one point of their star? (Too often this is a very large point!) Try selling that house little by little to free up cash for groceries. Some would argue that your primary residence is not an asset, but rather a liability; but that is another discussion!

Household diversification is a way to avoid putting all of our eggs in one financial basket. Everyone seems to agree with diversification, but all too often we have a very unbalanced portfolio. After all, we do not diversify because we think we know what is next, but rather because we have no idea what is next. The unexpected will be certain to arrive, so we should position ourselves to be ready. Diversify!

CHAPTER 9

THE HUMAN FACTOR IN FINANCE

*A*s you read this chapter you may find yourself saying, "Hey, I've said that before." You are not alone, for we are all somewhat a product of our environment. Each of the articles in this chapter are more about the philosophy of money than the making of money. We should never stop learning to be better people which ultimately helps us be better with money.

When I Get A Better Job...

I heard a silly little song the other day. It was called "If I Had A Million Dollars." The vocalists were listing all the crazy things they would do if they had a million dollars. Haven't you heard this money conversation before? It

121

seems like every party I have attended has at least one conversation that turns to money. Someone will bring up a very wealthy family's eccentric ways or the conversation will break into lottery fantasy. We probably have all had dreams of what to do with a large influx of money. It's a fun conversation. But, then the party ends, and Monday life returns to normal. If only there was more money we think, that would make life so much better, so much easier! Since the odds of winning the lottery are virtually zero we turn to a more practical approach and think, "If only I had a better paying job." If I had a better paying job, everything would be better. I would save more, spend money on my family and friends, become more generous, start my retirement saving, and on and on and on. So our hope is dependent on getting that better paying job...someday. No one would argue with that worthy goal, but we might have to admit that those we know who double their salary with a career move are few and far between. Unless we change our skill set dramatically through education/training etc. or move to another part of the country, an average raise is likely to be a conservative 3% to 5% per year, and the inflation cost may eat away 3% or 4% right off the top. This is starting to sound discouraging. Never fear. I contend that it is not the pay that needs a re-make but rather the financial philosophy itself. Perhaps the pay is fine (for now at least); it is our personal procurement department that brings our woes.

In their book *The Millionaire Next Door*, Thomas J. Stanley and William D. Danko give some interesting statistics about millionaires. Here are a few of their statistics, complete with my editorial comments!

1. The average is 57 years old (i.e. it takes a while.)

2. 95% are married. (They can not say their spouse spends too much!)

3. 80% are still working. (Even though they have a net worth over one million dollars.)

4. 66% are self-employed (Could this suggest they are self-starters?)

5. They are willing to pay for good investment advice. (They do not claim to have all of the answers.)

6. 95% of them own stock, yet they don't follow day to day movements of the market. (Could this suggest they are not trying to get rich tomorrow?)

7. They are goal oriented and spend ten hours monthly studying and planning the future. (They are not waiting for a better paying job.)

8. They spend money on family and grandchildren. (Their priorities are clear.)

9. They are very frugal. (Perhaps how they obtained wealth in the first place?)

It would appear to me that these folks have learned the critical laws of financial independence and have put them into practice.

How about you? How many of these qualities fit you? If financial independence is your goal, are you on your way?

Wrap it up, Kevin. If you can find a better paying job that fulfills you on a daily basis, I say go for it! However, I bump into so many folks that delay their financial future because they just know it will be so easy when that better paying job comes along, when their ship comes in, when they get these bills paid, when, when, when. As one friend of mine says, "it's not what you make, but what you keep!"

Over the years I have noticed in the money business that a person's household income does not necessarily determine their net worth. I have seen people who stock shelves invest a million dollars, or people in their twenties bring in more than some people ever save in a lifetime. It's not that hard to grow where you are planted. Develop good financial habits for <u>today's</u> income. And if that better job does come along? Great, you will have already established very good financial habits!

Remember to Watch Your Quality of Life

Not long ago I was on a red-eye flight on a small passenger jet with only one flight attendant. Have you noticed red-eye flights are full of folks just trying to get through the flight? Most people are tired and somber. Our attendant decided to enjoy our time together. He explained over the intercom that we could operate cell phones when the exit door was open, but the exit door is not usually open during the flight. He stated that "Should our flight turn into a cruise," there is a floatation device under your seat." He said to, "put it on and paddle!" He said, " Just in case you haven't ridden in an automobile since 1962," he would show us how a seat belt buckle was used. He also said that he was dimming the cabin lights, "to improve the appearance of the crew." He was certainly having a good time while he worked. He was either making the best of what he had or really loved his job. Either way, we all felt like we met a new friend. He took a group of tired people and had them laughing and clapping and enjoying life in the early hours of the morning.

Working is a good thing for most people. It gives a sense of purpose, helps our self esteem and gives us relationships and fulfillment which we all need (even if we don't admit we do.) Be careful with too much idle time in your schedule; you may be tempted to focus on yourself. Everyone can do something. When you change jobs, whether by your choice or not, look for that next job, which both uses your skills and improves your quality of life.

For example: I was talking to an early retiree. He was going to take a new job in his last few serious working years. We discussed a lot of ideas, but we looked specifically at building-in some quality of life items. For you, is it important to come to work at 10:00 am instead of 8:00 am? Perhaps you would enjoy Fridays off at noon or even Fridays off completely. Perhaps you would like 10 weeks of vacation. (Can you really afford more?). Perhaps you would like a company car in lieu of more pay, or even a bonus structure and no hours? Maybe you would not prefer to manage or maybe you prefer ONLY to manage. There are companies in the U.S. that even give a paid sabbatical of several weeks together after a number of years of employment. Employees can take their families on European vacations or other exotic bucket list adventures.

My dad used to say, "When you love your job, every day is pay day." He generally said this in jest when someone was complaining about their job, but the saying is really true. Find something where you are fulfilled and get paid for doing something you love. Many clients over the years have said I do (fill in the blank) and I can't believe I get paid for it!

One of the hardest questions you will ever be asked is, "What do you want to do." So many of us have a hard time really knowing what brings happiness.

There are many "perks" in any job that that would improve your quality of life. Pay is not the only factor!

Running Away And Running To

All too often I hear in one of our offices "I have to retire", or "I need to get out now, my job is literally driving me crazy" or "I'm going to explode from the stress of my job!", or "I don't know how long I can continue in this position, I don't care anymore". Most of these phrases will eventually become self-fulfilling prophecies. And I have learned that what the client is really saying is that they are trying their best to leave a stressful situation, they are running away from something painful. We try to help guide the decision making but all too often they just want out at any cost.

If you find yourself in just such a situation, try to seek wise counsel before you jump out of your job, especially if you are over age fifty. Older employees have a very difficult time replacing the pay and benefits of the old job, simply because they are older. A few months after they leave, they realize they gave up a lot in the hasty move and often never achieve the same level as before.

We usually recommend that a person hold the course until they can find something to "run to". Running "to" something is better than running "from" something! They stress may be great and you feel as though you cannot get out of there fast enough, but usually we only trade one stress for another when we leave abruptly. Use the stress to fuel your zeal for finding something fulfilling and THEN make your move with this in mind: Try your best to increase your quality of life in every change.

Sit down at the kitchen table and scribble down the ideal life situation. For example: You may say that having more vacation is better than more pay. A job that allows you to sit more and stand less may be desirable or you might like a job that allows you to get up and walk around instead of being stuck in a desk all day. Perhaps you would enjoy a career that has some travel required. What if you could have Friday off at noon or never had to work past 5 PM? What if you had use of a company car or worked the weekends and had two days off mid-week? What if you could work from home one day and could stay in your pajamas? What if you could take your dog to work or come in late after you dropped off your car for repair? Quality of life is different for individuals and what is valuable to one is not to another, so scribble down what would work best for you and then start planning.

We recommend to our clients that in each and every significant move they make in life whether it be a job, or a house or a career or a vacation home, moving to another state or just about anything else, we want them to facilitate things that INCREASE the quality of life for them. Think long and hard about the things that are valuable in life to you. America is one of the best places I know to foster thinking "outside of the box". Dream a little and start planning. Avoid running from something undesirable and start planning to run to something that increases your quality of life!

*A very powerful, intelligent, courteous, successful, high ranking military offi-
cer who had accomplished more in a month than many do in a decade once told
me, "Kevin, we must remember that we are but mere men." My own grandpa
rephrased this as, "Don't get too big for your britches." Perhaps doing what is right
should be in the first chapter because it is a foundation for all business, family and
social framework on finance. People of great character and integrity are a magnet
for prosperity.*

Doing What's Right Can Put
Money In Your Pocket

I know a fella that was in the contracting business. Call him Sam. He was
a good salesman but so were his competitors. A private business had asked
Sam's company to bid a very large contract. The stakes were high. During
the second bidding cycle, everyone was sharpening their pencils, so to speak.
Finally, the bids were opened but Sam was <u>not</u> the low bidder. And the low
bidder always gets the job right? Not this time. Something very interesting
happened.

The buyer had opened the second round of bids and was laboring over
the decision. He told his wife about the different competing companies and
she said, "I know Sam, but I haven't seen him in years!" she continued, "He
was always very honest and full of integrity." Case closed. The project was
awarded to Sam's company right then and there Why? The buyer now trusted
that Sam would do what was fair and equitable.

Honesty and integrity are great assets in the workplace. I believe that if
you practice them, word will get around. You just might profit from those
qualities because your reputation often arrives before you do and may count
for as many points as your bid price. Do what is right because it's better
business, because you'll be a better person, because you'll sleep better at night
and because your family will be proud of you. The side benefit is, it can put
money into your pocket!

One more thing: We all make mistakes in business. I have found that if I am up-front and honest about a goof and accept responsibility for it, the business relationship is rarely harmed and may even be strengthened.

Guard Your Reputation

A friend of mine says, "Guard your reputation; it is one of the best things you can have on your side." I think this is good advice, don't you? The same may be true in the world of finance. Your credit report is your financial reputation and it will likely make a significant difference in how you are treated and how much money you will ultimately make…or save.

Here is a real life, practical example. I have a client that opened his credit card statement and noticed a late charge and an over-limit fee posted to the account. After calling the credit card company, the customer service representative explained that the fees were indeed correct because the account was over the credit limit and the payment was a couple of days late. Although he did not like the charges, he was kind and understanding thanked the customer service representative and accepted their response. A few days later, something very interesting happened. The credit card company sent a hand written note saying they had removed both charges from the account, even though both were in accordance with the contract terms. I saw the note! But why had they done such a thing when they were clearly justified with their fees? Simple, he had a spotless credit record and paid his bill on time … usually. This time was an exception and the credit card company knew it was such. He had guarded his *credit* reputation.

Guarding your credit reputation can save you money. A good financial reputation will save you money on credit cards, car loans, home loans, and nearly every form of financing available. Your credit score will determine what type of terms you receive, which over the long haul can add up to thousands and thousands of dollars.

If you own a business, treat your credit reputation with kid gloves! Your suppliers will quickly learn your habits. No supplier wants to chase down their money. Often the business owner who pays on time gets the best prices, the best discounts, perks, priority on shipments, etc. Conversely, the slow paying account will be fortunate to get their goods. Be assured, they will receive the bare minimum. Haven't you heard that bad news travels fast? I believe the same is true with a poor credit reputation, especially in business.

So how about you? Are you bending the rules a bit on that bill? I know folks who pay their rent five days late every month. Why? I'm not sure. Eventually that ole habit will catch up to you. It would be wise to pay those bills on time or even a bit early to reverse the image that portrays. Two or three extra days of interest from the checking account while that bill goes late will have little impact on your long term net worth, but will have a certain impact on your credit score. If you lack the funds to pay bills a day or two early, chances are you are living beyond your means, and that is a dangerous game. Everyone can live on less. Every budget has something that can be trimmed. As always, delay no more, my friend. Start today. Want to check and see where your reputation stands? Here are three places to call for your credit report.

Equifax PO Box 740241 Atlanta, GA 30348, 1800-685-1111

Experian Inc., PO Box 9530, Allen, TX 75013, 1-888-397-3742

Trans Union Corp, PO Box 6790, Chester, Pa 19022, 1-800-888-4213

A Few Thanksgiving Ideas

We learned as youngsters that the Pilgrims celebrated Thanksgiving at Plymouth Rock about 1621, and now hundreds of years later we continue to follow this great tradition. For some it is a large gathering of friends and family. For others it can be a quiet time of reflection and gratitude. Hopefully for all of us it is a time to pause our normal routine for a short while to recall the good things in our lives, a *planned* time to be thankful and grateful. This year you might try a few of these Thanksgiving ideas.

Give something away. Send something at Thanksgiving…instead of at Christmas. We have all become accustomed to cards, letters, photos and even gifts at Christmas time. We may have even come to expect and anticipate them. But not at Thanksgiving! This year try sending out Thanksgiving cards. You could even send a Thanksgiving letter complete with a few pictures of your family and friends. Your letter will stand out because it's totally out of the ordinary and it really underlines the idea of being thankful. You could even give away a little of the bounty this year in that card. What a great time to start a college savings plan for one of the children in the family or fund a nest egg start for loved ones. If you have bounty, sharing it will enrich your own life as much or more than theirs.

Start some of your own family traditions. Traditions in a family can be a unifying foundation. For example, set a prescribed time each year to gather everyone and tell one or two things you appreciate about someone present. Too uncomfortable? Write them on a small card or paper and ask a senior family member to read them aloud. Allow only good things to be said. We all have our flaws and faults, but this is a time to dwell on everyone's strengths.

Attitude is everything. I think down deep inside most people realize that life in America is better than most places in the world. We have more opportunity, more money, more freedom, and more of anything anyone would want than anywhere in the world. But, we all get busy and distracted. After dinner ask your family's patriarch to lead a time of "thanksgiving." Ask people to share a few sentences about things they are thankful for. At first this may seem a bit awkward, but I believe you will find that once things get moving you might see some true emotions come out. You may see hearts soften with some real attitudes of thankfulness.

Pray together. Not your custom? Now is a great time to start. I think you will find that few people at your Thanksgiving table are looking for an eloquent dissertation. They will likely listen to your heart rather than your words, after all out of the overflow of the HEART the MOUTH speaks. This is an ideal time to get real, be honest, and publicly state your thankfulness.

Make Thanksgiving a day of celebration. Thanksgiving is a party, not a funeral. If you do not have conflicts, arguments or tensions on this day, consider yourself extra blessed. Many families do. If you expect trouble, address it right up front. As soon as everyone is assembled, spell out the rules of the game. If your house is the gathering spot make it clear that you will kindly ask offenders to leave and return when they are ready to celebrate with you. If it is not your turf, let them know that this is a time of thanksgiving for you, and if they fight, you are going to leave and celebrate elsewhere. Grudges don't work, but boundaries do!

Tax savings and giving at the same time. November is near the close of the tax year so why not start a scholarship fund in honor of someone dear. (You can honor someone that is at your table that day.) What a great surprise to announce that you have started a scholarship in their honor. Scholarships can be started at nearly any teaching institution. Be sure and check the tax code and the not-for-profit status if you expect a deduction. This can be a win-win-win situation. The recipient of your scholarship wins, the one that you donate on behalf of wins a great honor, and you win by receiving a tax deduction and great satisfaction as you share your blessings by giving to others.

Get More For Your Money...And Enjoy it.

Here are two great ways to save money without even trying. I think you'll find these interesting.

Be kind to people. Here is what I've discovered: every day in America, we bump into people in the marketplace, the grocery store, the gas station, at a restaurant, at a department store, on the phone to a customer service representative or even in a conversation with a telemarketer. We interact with people who are simply busy doing their job. Ask anyone who regularly works with the general public and they will tell you horror stories of how hard it is sometimes dealing with people who are upset, frustrated, stressed, worried etc. Stay with me, this is your cue! Make a special effort to be kind to these workers. You know how to be friendly when you want to be. Make up your mind that you will take the time, and decide to be cordial and pleasant, even when you feel they do not deserve this attitude from you. Then you will stand out in the crowd. Believe me, you WILL stand out. Watch how they respond. Not always, but more often than not you will get better service, better seats, better prices, fuller portions, upgrades, refills, coupons, certificates, promotional goods, suckers for your kids, doggie treats for the pooch, and a host of assorted freebies. Why? Because you were kind I have gotten countless hotel room upgrades for free, without requesting anything. My rental car has been upgraded "just because." My wife and I even got bumped to first class once on an airplane as a token of appreciation for being kind. Best of all, we did not ask for a thing. We reap what we sow.

And...secondly, be even <u>more</u> kind to unkind people. (You have to be kidding, right?) They need it! Often I find there is something running in the background that has nothing to do with you. They are grumpy because of a job issue, a family matter, worry, insecurity or the last customer that just chewed them out for something over which they had no control. You just happened to be the next customer in line.

The great part about practicing this philosophy is that you usually do not ever have to ask for a thing. They will just give it to you for being nice. These people are the employees. They have all the data. They know the product. They know how their company works and <u>they</u> really have the advantage. Being nice to them can get you a lot more for your money and you'll enjoy it! <u>Now don't be nice just to get something, or to save money. That is manipulation</u>. Be kind because it will make you a better person.

Alright, a little confession here. This is great advice, but I don't always use it. I have to admit, I become irritable sometimes and start snapping at folks. Then the reverse is true. These same employees give me the bare minimum in service and product. No one is going to go out of their way to help an ole grouch.

Try this some time to get you started: when you eat out and the waiter/ waitress does a great job, ask them to bring their manager back to your table so you can compliment them. A tired manager that has been solving problems all night will welcome your gesture. You'll make their day...and yours too!

It's Just Money...

My Father-in-law, "It's just money." He doesn't get too stressed about losses and doesn't get all that excited about gains. "Its just money," he says. I also have a friend that tells people "You'll never be truly happy until you are generous." I think they are both right.

Try this at home, think of five people you know. Maybe even scribble their names down and then rank them according to their generosity. Not always, but usually the one at the top of the generosity list is also enjoying life to the fullest. Other folks want to be around them. They are not intimidated. And if you watch, it just seems to come naturally to them. Now look at the bottom of your list. That bottom name probably stuck out in your mind. You know them, and may have befriended them but wish they were not that way. Words like cheap, miser, tightwad, squirrel, penny-pincher all come to mind. When I was very young, I had a friend who would fit that description. He always insisted we drive my car because he didn't have the money for gas. He was anything but generous. My car it was until the day he told me of the thousands and thousands of dollars stashed in his bank account. I never felt the same about driving my car or about my friend.

So how do you feel about that bottom name on your list? Do they make you feel uncomfortable? I'm not a psychologist, but it would appear to me that some people are just naturally generous and others have to <u>learn</u> these habits. Hold it. I'm not advising you to give away everything you own, but I am advocating generosity.

Many have to learn how to be generous. And when we finally do learn, it is rather hard to measure the amount of goodwill that will come our way as a result. Need some tips to get you started? Send a money order to someone you know needs the money. Don't tell you are the donor. Skip two meals and send the money to a homeless shelter or a rescue organization. Pay for dinner when it's really not your turn. If you see someone at the restaurant you know sitting at another table, send them dessert on your tab. Its just money! They'll never forget you (and neither will the person waiting on them). Next time you are at the store, look at the covers of the magazines or books and think of who you could send one in the mail. I think it will have a powerful impact. Gifts are an international sign of appreciation. Send a letter with it. After all, letters are also rare in our modern society. Learn to be generous. I'm not sure you'll ever be truly happy until you are. It's just money! Still not convinced? Think about this sobering thought: everything you own will eventually belong to someone else or be destroyed. You are only using your possessions for a time.

Someone once said that generosity is perhaps one of the hardest human emotion to conquer. Money is almost always connected in some way to our pleasure. Once the basic necessities are obtained, the left-over money really buys pleasure for the holder. So when we become generous, we are really forgoing a bit of our pleasure. It teaches us to put others needs before ourselves. We all love and care for ourselves daily. To put someone else above our own personal pleasure may be the opposite of human nature, but it is the essence of generosity.

Six Gifts

Once upon a time, long, long ago, in a land far, far away there was a young prince who was sent six gifts from six different people in his kingdom. Each gift was unique and fine, and, each gift bore the name of the bearer but gave no clues about the motives of the givers. The young prince was intrigued and wanted to know more about the givers, so he summoned his wise counselors and asked them to enlighten him about these gifts. This is what they said, "There are an infinite number of gifts, and givers, but only six reasons for giving."

1) <u>Guilt giving:</u> This giving is responsibility giving. A person gives because they "ought" to give. An example would be when you can hardly pay the bills

THE HUMAN FACTOR IN FINANCE

this month, Mr. And Mrs. Bixby (who you do not know well and have not seen in nine years) announce their daughter in Idaho is getting married… again. You feel guilty and send a gift in spite of your budget woes.

2) <u>Needs based giving</u>: You are in a food court waiting to place your order. There is a small girl in front of you who ordered French fries and is ten cents short. She doesn't find any more change in her pockets, and her mom is not in sight. You *willingly* provide the dime. The girl smiles, thanks you, and is on her way. You saw a need and gave accordingly and you have a big smile as you receive your order because you did something good.

3) <u>Abundance giving</u>: This is non-sacrificial giving. It is giving out of sheer abundance. I used to work for people who certainly had abundance and they routinely threw away items that were far better than anything I owned personally. A $50.00 bill to them was about like a quarter to me. This type of giving is really the overflow of a large cash stream. The giving of this gift changes nothing in the giver's life.

4) <u>Natural giving</u>: It seems some folks just give because it is their nature. Have you ever met someone who would give you anything they had? These people usually don't have much, don't need much and don't want much. They would rather give it away than keep it, just to see you smile. They give because they were born to give.

5) <u>Ulterior motive giving</u>: This is one to watch. Haven't you received this type of gift? It is usually nice, often it is even a sacrifice, but it always has strings attached. It might as well have a post-it note™ attached that says, "You owe us big-time now!" This gift will cost you in the long run. This gift will have an ulterior motive that usually becomes evident some time in the future.

6) <u>Joyous giving</u>: This is was giving with no strings attached. It is given because the giver wants you to know they love you, care about you, and want *you* to be happy and fulfilled. This type of gift is often a sacrifice on the part of the

donor. Furthermore it is given with a pure motive, and may be the "widow's mite." This gift is from the one who has mastered generosity. Even more, joyous giving benefits both the recipient and the donor. …And then the wise counselor said to the Prince, "My son you may try and determine which types of gifts you have here, but it is difficult to know the heart of the givers. Do not worry for this question is only a secondary concern. More importantly, you must determine what kind of giver are you?"

CHAPTER 10

COLLEGE LEVEL FINANCE/ THE APPENDIX

This chapter for many may be more of an appendix than a Sunday read. This gets deeper into our subject and will likely appeal to the engineer, physics teacher, or the technical professional. These articles build strong financial foundations.

What is Stock, Really?

It is 2:30 p.m. in St. Louis, and I have been asked twice already today what "stock" means and how it works. This may seem very simple to some, but to many, it is a confusing and complex system that rocks their financial world. Let me try to simplify the mechanics of the stock market. I'll not try and replace the university finance professors. Instead, I'll just barely skim the surface of stock market theory.

Let's use a hypothetical example. If the First Capital News (say FCN) were traded on the New York Stock Exchange (NYSE), then anyone (the public) could buy "shares" in that company. We will say the FCN decided to sell 1,000 shares at $10 per share. So, if you bought 15 shares you would own 15/1000ths of the company, in our case, the FCN. So what? How does one make money? Here are two common ways: 1) If the company (in our case FCN) were making money, they could pay a dividend to the shareholders. But, why would they do that? Well, since they are using the shareholder's money, they better pay them for that use. If there is no return provided, they will pull their cash out and put it into something else that <u>will</u> make a return. So since you own 15 shares, you would get a small amount (a dividend) for each share you own. Dividends are paid on a per share basis so each time the management declares a dividend, you would get paid based on the number of shares you own. 2) If the company is profitable, other people may want to buy the stock. But remember, there are only 1000 shares and you own 15 of them. You many not want to sell them if the company has been very loyal about paying you that dividend. Or, maybe you have no use for the cash right now. Hence, supply is lower and demand is higher. Therefore the stock price may rise. Later the stock price rises to $12.50 per share, and you decide to sell your stock. You have made $2.50 for each share you own, and of course you are returned your original $10 per share as well. This is a simple profit made by an increase in the price.

But, what happens if the company does poorly? Or in other words, they have very little earnings and the stock price drops to say $8 per share. Now, if you sell, you have lost $2 for each share you own. You do not have to sell right now (this is called a paper loss if you do not.) But if you do, then you would lose $2.00 for each share you own. Of course you could keep the stock in anticipation of an increased price in the future.

If we were to stroll through the local retailer's shop, we all understand when we see statements like: on sale, red tag sale, marked-down, clearance item and so on. But when we flip on the nightly television news and watch the floor of the New York Stock Exchange where floor traders yell and sell we see no "red-tag sale" signs. Stock prices change daily so folks sometimes get puzzled trying to figure out when they should buy and sell. Stock prices may change hundreds of times per day, and often very quickly. The stock price of one company may change all day long and close higher or lower than the previous day. So how do we tell if a stock is on sale or marked up? Often we will look at the price to earnings ratio (PE) to give us a quick insight as to the stocks popularity...a quick look at the supply and demand. We will save this discussion for another time! In the mean time, now we understand two ways to make or lose money in the ole stock market.

What's The PE Ratio?

Do you remember the commercial that was on television showing a father sitting at his computer impressing his family with technical words and phrases like "book value", "beta", "sigma" and "debt to equity ratios"? The father was obviously quite pleased with his newly acquired financial vocabulary. Just then his little boy asks, "Daddy, what's a PE ratio?" (one of the most basic ratios in equity finance). The father gets a dumbfounded look of fear because he knows nothing about the stock market, his investments, or PE ratios! He was simply using financial terms to impress. While you may not aspire to be a great financial guru, the little boy's question about PE ratios is a pretty good one. In my opinion, if you are going to own stock, it might be a good idea to know something about stock!

Mark Twain is credited with saying, "OCTOBER: This is one of the peculiarly dangerous months to speculate in stocks. The others are July, January, September, April, November, May, March, June, December, August, and February."* I think Mark Twain knew that many people were just like the man in that popular commercial.

If we divide the price of the stock by the earnings of the company we get an idea of how much investors may be willing to pay for a slice of a particular company.

The price-to-earnings ratio (PE ratio for short) is perhaps one of the most popular rules of thumb that students of the stock markets use. The PE ratio is to the investor what the hammer is to the carpenter. This price-to-earnings ratio is just what it says, a ratio of a particular stock's price compared to the earnings that same stock provides.

If we divide the price of the stock by the earnings of the company (data that is readily available on thousands of web sites), we can know how much investors are currently willing to pay for a slice of this particular company.

The father in our television commercial could have responded to his child that PE may be insightful for determining if the public considers a stock "on sale" or "overpriced" and by how much. A PE ratio of 77, by definition, means the price of the stock is 77 times the earnings of the company. Also by definition a PE ratio of 77 means that the earnings are 1/77th of the price of the stock. We get this through simple division.

So we can walk away with this: By definition, *High* PE ratios mean folks are willing to pay more for a stock (for some reason). *Low* PE ratios tell us that folks are unwilling to pay more for these earnings (for some reason).

In my experience, many people that own stock have almost no knowledge of what that stock is worth. Would you buy a car, or a house with no idea of it's value? Understanding PE ratios is one way to help determine how valuable a particular stock is to the investing public. It is certainly not the all inclusive answer, but it can be a quick, shoot-from-the-hip rule of thumb that helps build your case for or against candidacy in your portfolio. *Pudd'nhead Wilson's Calendar*

What Is An ETF?

Ask a veteran of the financial world how long it takes to completely master the field of finance and they will tell you that one never does know all there is to know. Like many technical fields, finance is ever changing and growing. In recent years we have seen an explosion of ETFs or exchange traded funds use in portfolios. This article is intended to be a "light overview" of the vast world of this new tool.

Today the typical investor is familiar with mutual funds and understands that the mutual fund is a way to diversify a portfolio over many underlying individual stocks. Exchange traded funds are not so readily understood. Let me try and give a quick understanding of these new investment vehicles that seem to be ever growing and expanding in variety and popularity.

As a general rule ETFs have significantly lower costs than mutual funds. They are not managed and therefore, there is no manager to pay a recurring fee.

Tax Efficiency: Mutual funds must pay out dividends and capital gain every year. When a shareholder redeems a mutual fund, the fund has to liquidate shares to provide cash for payout. This means something has to be sold and therefore there is a capital gain or loss. Even when a portfolio is down for the year, the owner of the fund can still have to pay capital gains because the underlying stocks that were sold (to provide the cash) were sold at a profit. This creates a tax burden for all shareholders. Furthermore, they have to pay out dividends and capital gains every year, which can lead to a tax bill even when the fund was negative for the year. ETFs can trade in kind, which means stock for stock. So they do pay capital gains unless they are changing the basket of stocks. Over 90% of ishare ETFs generally pay no capital gains.

Rapid buying and selling: Remember ETSs are EXCHANGE traded funds, i.e. they sell on the open market and are subject to market fluctuations throughout the day (mutual are priced at market close.) We said that freeing up cash in a mutual fund was accomplished through redeeming shares or telling the fund manager to liquidate some stock positions to allow the shareholder to receive their cash. ETFs do not sell to the fund manager, they trade the shares they want to sell on the open market to someone who wants to buy. This makes an ETF extremely liquid.

Generally we think of ETFs as replicators of indexes like the popular Diamonds Trust Series (DIA) for example, an ETF that is designed to model the Dow Jones Industrial index. Now, they can be made to emulate a specific sector as well. China, India, precious metals, commodities, real estate would be just a few examples. The focus of these funds can be nearly endless. Furthermore, they can be passively managed or actively managed.

Rebalancing of the ETF: During the year, ETFs can develop what is called trade inefficiencies through drifting of the underlying holdings. Usually mid year the fund will correct this trade error by a comparison to the index that is being replicated and rebalancing.

Many would hold that if an index type ETF was very broad based, it would provide great diversification. But remember it could be used with very specific holdings. Opponents would say that this encourages short term investing.

If you believe that active management outperforms static ETFs over the long run, ETFs would be better for shorter time frames, or be included as part of an ETF managed portfolio. ETFs tend to perform better in a down market because of the broad based of an index. Mutuals are better on the up side because the manager can be more weighted in a specific sector of the market and if they are right, they will out perform. Generally ETFs replicate an index by owning the individual stocks

Why Roll over?

It seems like everywhere we see financial literature there are advertisements talking about "rollovers." Even financial offices have on their window, "We do rollovers." What is a rollover, and what is all of the rollover commotion about?

Usually when someone leaves their place of employment, they have the choice of "rolling" their company savings plan assets "over" to another plan. A rollover. Not all, but some company plans require that the money be rolled over within a certain time period. Many plans will allow the assets to remain in the old employer's program but there are often advantages and disadvantages to moving the funds out. One significant disadvantage is that generally, people who leave their employer plan after age 55 might be able to withdraw from a plan without penalty. This is not true in an IRA. Another disadvantage might be an old fixed rate or guaranteed income contract that will give you a higher fixed interest than you could receive in an IRA.

Here are a few possible <u>advantages</u> of a rollover, or the moving of retirement funds out of your old employer's plan:

- ✓ Allows you to consolidate assets from several different accounts such as pensions, 401(k) plans, etc. which can simplify reporting paperwork.

- ✓ May allow you to withdraw money from your account via monthly checks.

- ✓ May give you a broader investment choice as opposed to those picked by the employer

- ✓ Gives the owner ultimate control

- ✓ Allows funds to be moved to other investments (provided it remains in a traditional IRA account).

- ✓ May allow special benefits such as reduced or waived annual fees.

- ✓ Maintains the tax-deferred status of a 401(k) account.

- ✓ Usually allows withdrawal of funds without IRS penalties provided the recipient is older than 59 1/2.

- ✓ Once rolled into a traditional IRA, may be eligible for conversion to a Roth IRA. Employer plans cannot be converted to Roth IRAs.

- ✓ Allows your beneficiaries to "stretch" the IRA according to their life expectancy, most 401(k)s do not allow this.

- ✓ Typically withdrawals are easier in an IRA than a 401(k)

- ✓ Rollovers aggregate Required Minimum Distributions where 401(k)s do not.

- ✓ These are great reasons but in my mind the biggest reason for starting a rollover is control. When you roll funds into a traditional IRA, you have control over the management of your funds. No one cares more about your money than you do, so why shouldn't you have the control? You then have the choice of who will help you, or if you will even need help.

Another point to note is this: In cases where the employee decides to get another job, the officials of the new employer's retirement savings program will recommend that the money be immediately transferred into their plan. Beware my friend, this usually means these funds are then bound by the rules and regulations of the new plan and will NOT be eligible for another rollover until you are no longer employed by that new company. This could be a very long time! Furthermore, if the employer changes providers, the rules governing your money will likely change as well. So if you have an old 401(k) or employer plan, you may want to consider a rollover soon.

One word of caution: I have had clients who checked the wrong box on the transfer paperwork, which generated a liquidation check. They did not realize that this started a time clock. If they are not expedient about their new home for the money, the IRS grace period could lapse which creates an <u>irrevocable</u> tax consequence with the Internal Revenue Service. Yikes! If you are unsure or you get a check in the mail, do not cash it until you get professional assistance! The IRS will not be interested in your explanation.

Constantly in client meetings we discuss the difference in tax treatment and investment. Even savvy investors get them confused. When someone asks how much a Roth IRA makes we might jest and say how high does your dog fly? Neither make sense. Dogs don't fly (at least today) and Roth IRAs don't make anything. Rather, the term "Roth IRA" describes the tax treatment of the account, not the investment itself.

Two Types of Money

There are two types of money and you can have both.

It seems like more often than I care to admit, at the end of what I *thought* was an eloquent, prepared and very clear explanation of the investment process, someone will ask how much an Individual Retirement Account (IRA) makes. I realize that either I failed to explain about the two types of money or it did not sink in when I did. Either way, they missed the point. Every account has a tax treatment and an investment component.

Regarding tax treatments there are two basic types of money: 1) non-qualified and 2) qualified. Your account is one or the other. But qualified by what? As the name suggests qualified accounts are qualified by something or someone, usually Uncle Sam. The government puts restrictions or qualifications on IRAs to encourage savings and to discourage spending (before retirement.) Conversely, non-qualified money is, just as the name implies, not-qualified by something. It is really easy to remember either "qualified"…by something and "non-qualified"… (or not-qualified) by something.

Let's look at some examples. A 401(k) account, an IRA, a 403(b) and a college savings account, are all examples of qualified money. There are restrictions concerning when you can withdraw the money and to what use it can be put. On the other hand, money in your checking account is an example of non-qualified funds because you can spend that money anytime you like on whatever you please. Easy right?

Now try this: your dear Auntie gives you $5,000 for you birthday (whew, nice Aunt!) When you deposit the money is it qualified or non-qualified? The answer is either one, because you make that choice. If you put the money into an IRA it will become qualified by the US government (by law). But if you put that $5,000 in an account titled as non-qualified, then you could use the money as you please just as if it were in a checking account. *A key point to remember is that qualified and non qualified has nothing to do with how or where the money is invested, what rate of return it will yield, or if it will yield a return at all.*

So there you have the two types of money. Both have specific purposes and which type the money will be is your choice when you elect where it will be held, including some of both.

Understanding An Index

Not long ago, my eight year old daughter was singing in the car. In the middle of the song she added, "E-minor!" After two or three times, I inquired about this random phrase being thrown into an otherwise normal song. She said, "I don't know what it means, but you say it when you are leading the band." (She was referring to a band practice I had having a few weeks earlier.) She was using the term, yet had no idea what it meant.

Similarly, someone will chide, "The market's down today." Yet, sometimes have very little understanding of what it really means for the market to be down. They just know it gets a response from those in earshot. Let me see if I can help. The Dow Jones Industrial Average (DJIA or $IND) is comprised of 30 stocks in many different industries that are intended to be a model of the market as a whole. Usually when someone says the market is up, they are referring to the DJIA*. Similarly, the S & P 500 (Standard and Poors 500) or the NASDAQ (National Association of Securities Dealers Automated Quotation) would be runners-up in popular indices. Clip this list for reference:

DJIA – Large Industrial US Stocks

153

S&P500 – General Market Performance of Large Common US Stocks

NASDAQ – Tracks the Over-the-Counter Common Stocks. Often Used For "Tech" Stocks

Wilshire 5000 – Broad Index Of 5000 US Corporations

Russell 2000 – Measures Small Capitalization Stocks

MSCI EAFE – Morgan Stanley Capital International Index. Measures stocks of Europe, Australia, Asia and Far East.

LB Agg – Lehman Brothers Aggregate Bond Index

Each of these tries to accurately model how that piece of the market responded to investor trading. The key here is to understand what the numbers are telling you*. Try these two basic uses: first, look at an index benchmark and compare that number to today's value. For example: right after September 11th, 2001, the DJIA was approximately 8500 points. So, if the DJIA were at 9000 points one year later, we could say the market had a 5.9% gain over that period. (9000/8500 = 1.059). If the DJIA were still 8500 points after that year, then you could say the market as a whole had no gain over that span. However, it is important to note that this does not mean your individual stocks or mutual funds had no gain or loss. Remember, indices MODEL what the market does collectively. It is designed to give you a quick overview. Hence, an index <u>fund</u> mirrors as closely as possible the index itself.

Secondly, look at changes in the averages to determine the direction of the market. For example: if on Monday the NASDAQ was 1400 points and Tuesday it was down to 1360, this is a 3% drop (1- 1360/1400). If we looked at the trend over a few weeks, we may begin to see a pattern. The direction of the market becomes obvious.

The punch-line: the direction of the markets and the overall profit or loss of the markets can be determined from these very valuable indices. I think you will also find it interesting that every investment you have will list an index to use as the performance gauge. This can be easily found on the internet or in your prospectus. Look for one of the indices we listed and start watching how it moves. You won't have to ask if your investments dropped on a given day. You will have a really good idea just from the index that your investment follows.

* The DJIA is a weighted average of 30 different stock prices. The key is not how the calculation is made but rather how the index moves to a given stimulus.

Certainly the IRS must have countless cases of well intentioned individuals who did not understand the terminology of their plan paperwork and incorrectly moved money. Later they discover a tax consequence or a mistake that may last for a lifetime or have irrevocable consequences. These are terms you will likely use only a few times in your investment career, but you either have to understand them or hire someone that does.

Trustee-to-Trustee Transfers, 1035s, and Rollovers

You could read the title of this article and think, "Who cares?" But if the Internal Revenue Service (IRS) were to come asking questions about your tax return, you might develop a new found interest! If not done correctly, simple financial transactions on retirement money can trigger a taxable event, which might just mean the IRS is going to want tax money!

Let's consider the 1035 first. A 1035 exchange, by definition, could simply be transferring funds from one life insurance product to another, typically an annuity. This is from Section 1035 of the tax code and is simply a way to allow an owner to transfer from one insurance product to another without creating a taxable event. As new products with new features enter the marketplace, often consumers feel that an alternate product better suits their needs. So, the IRS allows the owner to transfer money within certain parameters. (Of course there may also be sponsor related fees and charges that may not make this advantageous for the consumer.)

> *...a trustee-to-trustee transfer moves money directly from one custodian to another without the owner being in the middle.*

Often an employee leaves a company yet has retirement funds still remaining in the company retirement plan. In the industry. passing funds from one trustee to another is called a trustee-to-trustee transfer or a direct transfer. It is important to note that the money <u>bypassed the owner's bank account</u>, as it went from one trustee to another with the intent of deferring taxation. We could say that a trustee-to-trustee transfer moves money directly from one custodian to another without the owner being in the middle. Again, the money transfers from one custodian (eg. the old 401K provider) to the new custodian (eg. the new traditional IRA provider). This is an effective way to move money from one eligible retirement plan to another while keeping the owner out of the loop so the IRS does not need to be involved.

So what is a true rollover (that uses the 60-day rule)? It is a transfer where the owner *does* get in the middle. In this situation the owner can deposit earmarked retirement funds into their bank account for a period of time. Be careful here, there are three important rules that, if not followed explicitly, could trigger tax due and possibly penalties*. The rules are: 1) there are only 60 days allowed to transfer funds back to a new receiving custodian and 2) when you make the withdrawal the custodian will withhold 20% for taxes. If you do not replace the 20% required withholding within the 60 day period, you will be taxed on the withholding and you may be subject to the 10% withdrawal penalty depending on the owner's age. 3) Finally: you can only do this once per year. A direct rollover is the most common way to transfer from an employer plan to an IRA and it does not involve the 60-day rule. As a result of this rollover grace period, some of the public have attempted to use this as a temporary 60-day loan. This is an unforgiving scenario and I strongly recommend understanding IRS rules prior to undertaking such an endeavor!

So, there are three little terms and three big topics to help you stay out of the turbulent sea of taxation!

*See irs.gov for specifics

Source: IRS.gov

Annuities and Annuitization

It seems that all too often I see a glazed-over look on client faces when I speak of annuities, payment streams, annuitization or living benefits. I think most of the glazed look comes from an overload of unfamiliar terminology. Like every profession, we become comfortable with our industry jargon and acronyms, and the client (who probably could not care less) starts thinking about what they want to eat for lunch instead of attempting to de-code the conversation. In the end, some of them start believing that they will have to give all of their money to the insurance company only to die a few months later, thereby robbing their heirs of all inheritance.

...the word annuity is NOT another word for annuitizing.

The mechanics of an annuity are certainly beyond the scope of this article but please understand that the word annuity is NOT another word for annuitizing. Many times when we say *annuity*, folks hear or believe we mean *annuitization*.

Let me take a moment to clear the confusion on these two similar terms. First "annuity." Just like the word "vehicle" describes hundreds of makes and models of every sort of car and truck imaginable, the word "annuity" is a broad term that describes hundreds of packaged products used for building wealth. They have been around since the days of the Roman Empire.

Most vehicles, while quite different than each other, and quite unique in their individual features, are for the purpose of transporting people from one place to another. Likewise, annuities, while quite different from each other, and quite unique in their individual features, are fort the purpose of building or distributing wealth. Typically annuities have two parts: an accumulation part or phase when the goal is to gather assets, and a withdrawal phase where the owner begins to take distributions from the accumulated value.

"Annuitization," or "annuitizing," means to convert a sum of money into an equal periodic stream of payments that last for a specified (and contractual) period of time. The period of time can be a number of years, a lifetime or two lifetimes. You *can* annuitize an annuity, but you certainly are not required to do such a thing. (Folks routinely think annuities must be annuitized.)

Why would anyone need a contract annuitized? Well, let's suppose someone has a farm and a large farmhouse, (illiquid assets) yet lives alone and needs to hire services like mowing, car maintenance, etc. They could liquidate a portion of their assets and annuitize the money in order to create a stream of income for as long as they live to help with those expenses.

Furthermore, most modern immediate annuities (which are annuitized) have what is called a return of premium." This is a feature that, in case of an untimely death of an owner, allows the premium or amount paid to be returned to someone even though the owner is deceased. Hence, the language "with return of premium."

So watch the two words, "annuity" and "annuitize." They are very, very different.

Congratulations. You have reached the end of this book on finance. I sincerely hope that you think differently now about your financial future than you did when you started. If so, goal attained! If nothing else, focus on the human factor in finance. Focus on doing what is right and noble. This will build a great foundation for every event in your life and I believe you will be surprised at how many wonderful financial things will simply unfold with very little effort. If we can ever be of assistance, don't hesitate to call.

ALL PROFITS FROM THE SALE OF THIS BOOK GO TO CHARITY